Best regards,
Diane M. marobella

Haunted by the Spirit

By

Raffaele J. Bibbo and Diane M. Marobella

Best Wishes
Raffaele J Bibbo

ISBN: 1-4033-9679-5 (e-book)
ISBN: 1-4033-9680-9 (Paperback)
ISBN: 1-4033-9681-7 (Dust Jacket)

Library of Congress Control Number: 2002096055

This book is printed on acid free paper.

Printed in the United States of America
Bloomington, IN

1stBooks - rev. 02/26/03

Dedication

This book is dedicated to all the souls who departed the physical plain and are searching for answers beyond the realm of our understanding. May God help you find the way and surround you with his love.

Table of Contents

Dedication iii

ABOUT THE BOOK ix

« I »

The Funeral 1

« II »

First Meeting with Rebecca 5

« III »

Rebecca Attends First Weight Class 10

« IV »

Rebecca's Introduction to the Spirit World 15

« V »

Doris Speaks 23

« VI »

The Host Body Regains Composure 45

« VII »

Research & Review of Data...55

« VIII »

A Blast from the Past..63

« IX »

The Victim Returns...70

« X »

Doris Begins Her Revenge..93

« XI »

The Plot Thickens..96

« XII »

Life on the Plantation...109

« XIII »

Rebecca & Millie Meet Again..126

« XIV »

A Time to Reflect...130

« XV »

Elimination of Suspects... 140

« XVI »

Rebecca Reaches Out 148

« XVII »

The Torment Continues.. 153

« XVIII »

Trouble for Rebecca... 160

« XIX »

The Cover Up.. 166

« XX »

Raffaele Meets with the Police 179

« XXI »

Doris Lets the Cat Out of the Bag 184

« XXII »

Guess Who's Coming to Dinner.. 193

« XXIII »

Doris's Last Day on Earth.. 201

«XXIV»

A Dying Woman's Confession.. *215*

About the Author.. *229*

ABOUT THE BOOK

HAUNTED BY THE SPIRIT ©2000

BY
Raffaele J. Bibbo
Diane M. Marobella

This story is about an unsolved murder that was committed on August 16, 1967 in the City of Waltham, Massachusetts, near the Weston town line about 10 miles west of Boston. The partially clad body of a 48-year old woman was found with no shoes on and one of her silk stockings wrapped around her neck, strangling her to death.

This presentation is based on a true story with unsolicited revelations making an accusation from beyond the grave. Was the truth of what happened generated by the spirit of the deceased or was it from guilt that haunted the murderer into a confession? As the story unfolds and the sequence of events are revealed, it will hold you in suspense as it leads up to the actual murder of the young lady. According to the Waltham police, this murder case is considered as a "cold case" (unsolved to date). You be the judge. Is this case still unsolved or has it been resolved thirty-three years later?

The authors first received their information in 1984 through a séance in which an unknown entity unexpectedly entered the body of the alleged murderer. This entity shouted to all those present, **"This body murdered me!"** At a later date, the voice identified to be none other than the deceased, Doris A. Johnson. Did the deceased come back in spirit and control the killer into a confession thirty-three years later, or was the killer's own guilt overcome by its own spirit into revealing the truth that she could not hold back anymore?

Bear in mind, we are all living spirits having a human experience until such time when death occurs and the soul departs the physical body, thus becoming an integral part of the spiritual world..

« *I* »

The Funeral

It was mid-morning on May 17, 1990, it was cold and felt like it was going to rain. A chill went through my body as I stood at the top of the hill looking down at the cemetery gates. Looking further up the road, I could see the funeral procession slowly approaching the entrance. As the hearse turned through the gates and made its way toward the final resting place, I began to reminisce about my acquaintance with the deceased.

I met Rebecca approximately six years ago, and the last time I saw her was about a month ago when I visited her in the hospital. She had a terminal illness, and it was only a matter of time before we would all be gathered here to pay our last respects. As the funeral procession moved its way slowly through the narrow roadway up to the gravesite, I began to wander in thought. To what part of God's Kingdom has her soul departed?

As I pondered upon this question, I could hear the priest as he recited the burial rites. "The body would return to the ground from which it came, ashes to ashes, dust to dust, but the soul will return to God." It became apparent to me that this soul could be lost in limbo indefinitely or remain earthbound if what she revealed was true. I have always believed that we have one corporeal body on this earth, and how we live from day to day depends solely on the choice of the individual's lifestyle and morals.

For over twenty-five years, Rebecca lived in this city, and in that span of time she was involved with many activities and had made a multitude of friends as well as enemies.

As the clouds began to move in, I felt a drizzly mist starting to fall, and a cold chill once again shot through my body. The fog slowly drifted in, and it created an eerie mood. The priest completed the burial rites, and friends and acquaintances of Rebecca started to move out. I walked over to the site, plucked a flower from one of the wreaths and tossed it on the lid of the coffin. I mentally spoke to Rebecca.

"Well Rebecca, it's been over six years since you told me not to write your story until death came and took you away." I don't know if I felt sorry that she had passed on or if it was a relief, for I only had to wait five more years to write her story.

As I drove back to my office, my mood was such that I did not want to return to work. I wanted to reflect back and think about Rebecca's amazing story. I accidentally came upon this unsolicited story, and I was sure the time would come when I could reveal it. Where would I start? How could I reveal the story without hurting anyone? Rebecca still had living family members. I wondered if they knew what I had uncovered. The story has to be told.

« *II* »

First Meeting with Rebecca

Upon arriving at my office, I found it empty because my surveyors and engineers were in the field working. This seemed to be an opportune time to meditate. I let my body fall into the comfortable easy chair behind my desk, took a deep breath, and closed my eyes. I became aware that the rain was now falling harder, and the monotonous sound of the rain drops helped to put me in a relaxed hypnotic state, where I could think back in time to that day when I received a phone call from Rebecca's friend. She told me that a friend of hers was in dire need of some help, and she believed I might be able to assist her. She asked if an appointment could be arranged for her friend to meet me in my office one night during the coming week. I told the caller to bring her friend to my office the following week so we could have a talk.

At this time, I had no idea who this person was or what her reason was for wanting to see me. Many people call me for help because of my expertise in hypnosis which I use for behavior modification, memory recall, or to recover a lost item or article.

In the first week of January 1984, while working late at my office, the doorbell rang. Upon opening the door, there stood before me a rather large, massive woman. She appeared to be at least six feet tall and about 250 pounds in body weight. She had long, sandy blonde hair and was shabbily dressed. This woman looked like an Amazon. She shoved her hand forward to grasp mine and shook it while saying, "Hi, I'm Rebecca. Are you Raffaele?" She had a very strong handshake and gripped much like a man.

I said, "Yes, I am. Come on in and have a seat. Tell me, how can I help you?"

She proceeded to tell me that she had heard numerous stories about the success of my weight loss program and the innovative techniques of how I use hypnosis to help people lose weight. She told me she was in dire need to lose fifty or more pounds and wanted to know if my method could help her shed the fat off her body as successfully as some of my other clients whom she claimed to know. I proceeded to ask her a series of questions in order to find out how receptive she could be, and, at the same time, it gave me an opportunity to study her. She seemed to be very jittery, nervous, and unusually tense.

She made many irregular movements with her body. For instance, she rubbed her hands, shifted her eyes, crossed her legs, rocked her body, and turned from side to side. All of this indicated that she was very nervous. She was not a pretty woman and appeared to be more on the masculine side. Her attire consisted of ratty blue jeans, a grubby tee shirt, and dirty sneakers minus the socks. Her long blonde hair was tied back, and she was not wearing any makeup. Her tee shirt was somewhat damp, and it was obvious that she was not wearing a brassiere. Her tone of voice indicated a southern accent, and, at a later date, it was confirmed that she was born in a southern state. She told me she was married and had two children.

Rebecca looked at her watch and said, "Wow, it's getting late. Quickly tell me something about your program. I have to go." After she listened to what I had to say about the program that incorporated the use of hypnosis, she was fascinated and said that she had always wanted to be hypnotized. She claimed that she always volunteered at nightclubs to go up on stage in an attempt to be hypnotized, but it always failed. (Facetiously, I thought to myself that she might have frightened the hypnotist). She believed that she could not be hypnotized, but was willing and anxious to try. Reluctantly, I scheduled her for my next weight class.

She stood up, shook my hand like a man, and said, "I'm looking forward to this class. I'll see you next week." She continued, "If you can put me to sleep, you'll be the first."

As she left, I said to myself, "This will be like trying to put Ma Baker to sleep."

« *III* »

Rebecca Attends First Weight Class

The following week she brought a friend with her to keep her company and asked me if her friend could sit in on the class. I said it was okay. Her wardrobe did not seem to improve from our last meeting, and her friend was not dressed any better.

I usually hold evening classes for about fifteen people at a time. I always lecture for the first ten to fifteen minutes to set the tone or mood to help my clients relax. I kept my eye on Rebecca so I could determine how she was responding. Being a big woman, she filled the seat and seemed to watch my every movement. I have a habit of pacing back and forth in front of the class when I lecture; thus, my clients' eyes follow me back and forth as if a pendulum was swinging helping to create a trance-like state.

It was now time for me to place the headphones on the clients and prepare them to be receptive to my lecture under the state of hypnosis. This would help them retain the weight loss suggestions from this point on and up to the next class. Rebecca responded fantastically. She had an immediate rapport and drifted into hypnosis as if going into a deep sleep. She was receptive to all of the suggestions in preparation for the coming week. She was eager to eat less and think positive about herself as if she was already slender, healthy, and beautiful.

Over the next several weeks of classes, Rebecca had tremendous success. She was losing weight at a clip of three to five pounds a week. It was so noticeable that Rebecca was starting to wear more appropriate expensive clothing, and she had her hair styled and began to wear a little makeup. I felt this was a good sign, as Rebecca was taking pride in herself. Despite her size, her appearance took on a whole new meaning. One night, upon completing a class, Rebecca asked me why some clients remained after the weight class ended. I explained to her that I had a special class in which I conducted experiments regarding the spiritual world – a so-called psychic world in reference to life after death. She thought that sounded fascinating and asked if she could remain to witness a program. I had no objection and told her to keep an open mind to whatever she hears or sees. It just so happened that I was doing some research with a volunteer who was a superb subject. This subject accepted a trance condition to the extent of allowing her conscience mind to become arrested, thus allowing the subconscious mind to open up and allow a temporary spirit possession of her body. This is where the body and mind become completely susceptible and cooperative where it seems that an outside entity would make an entry. It could be an energy form or an ethereal spirit form that would temporarily take over the body and attempt to communicate with us.

I had been practicing and experimenting along this line for over some thirty years since I got out of high school in 1951. Rebecca watched in awe and participated by asking many questions. Because of her curiosity, she wanted to know if she could have a chance and sit in the head chair to see if this could work for her. Rebecca's friend told us we were both out of our minds to be involved with this and said she did not want to have any part of it, now or at any time. Rebecca did not care what her friend thought and said she would like to try it the next time she was here. She seemed eager, willing, and excited about this, so I told her that at the end of next week's class, if she still felt the same way, I would only test her out to see if she could become receptive to allow a spirit possession to enter her body and become one. We then sat around and had coffee and discussed the events that took place that night.

« *IV* »

Rebecca's Introduction to the Spirit World

The following week, Rebecca came to class alone. She was smartly dressed and looked good, and she was proud that she had shed over thirty pounds of fat from her body. She accepted the fact that this was a night out with people who shared the same condition such as obesity and the same interest into the realm of the psychic world or spiritual world, always hoping that some truth would come forth where it could be verified.

My main interest is specifically in the area of what happens when the body dies. Is that the end or does something else take place? I believe, without a doubt, that when the body dies, the essence of the individual does live on. No matter what the scientists, scholars, or theologians call it, something still exists. If everything in the universe has a purpose, then what would be the purpose of man acquiring knowledge, intelligence, and wisdom from the moment of birth up to the moment of death? Therefore, the continuation of what man has established for himself must continue, otherwise his life is a waste. Upon completion of one's education, the usual daily routine is merely to get up in the morning, eat breakfast, go to work, eat lunch, go back to work, leave work for the day, go home, eat dinner, and go to bed only to wake up the next morning to start this cycle all over again. This cycle continues throughout your life until the body expires without realizing that something continues after death. Let's assume the continuation of life after death can be referred to as the soul or the essence of the individual.

At the conclusion of weight class, everyone left except those who participated every week with the psychic class.

We had some coffee and wasted a few more minutes because I was expecting some guests to sit in on the session. As usual, I had the tape recorder set up to make a copy of what would transpire. There were approximately fifteen people present as witnesses to keep notes or ask questions.

The date of March 8, 1984 and the time being 10:00 P.M. will forever be remembered. It was on this date and time that the unforgettable chain of events began. There seemed to be a mystique aura, and some of the witnesses were jittery. Patiently, everyone waited for the session to begin. I must admit that Rebecca was very calm and not excited like the majority of subjects who attempted this method of spiritual possession.

She sat very comfortably in the easy chair and placed her arms on the armrest. I asked her how she felt. She told me that she was very relaxed and felt good. I asked my associate to hand me the small bottle that was on the table

17

and to start the tape recorder. The small bottle contained holy water that I constantly used in all of my sessions, whether the subject was a believer or a disbeliever in the faith of God through the Catholic Church.

I placed the holy water on her forehead and made the sign of the cross. While doing this, I asked Rebecca to close her eyes, take a deep breath, and exhale very slowly. As this was being done, I recited my opening remarks, as I have always done prior to each session. "In the name of my Creator, the Father most high and through his Son, my Master, Jesus Christ, in communion with the Holy Spirit, I ask for that what we are about to experience to be safe for the one with whom we are working and those present. Further, if it pleases you, let us learn from this event if it is to be successful."

Over the years, I have found that if I ask for things in Jesus' name, and it is not intended to hurt anyone, the results are usually successful. I did not know what to expect from this night or from anyone with whom I worked. It is not my intent to pry into anyone's personal life or problems, but somehow tonight felt different. The room seemed much quieter, and, if a pin were to drop, it would sound like a big bang. Rebecca responded immediately and drifted into a deep sleep. You could see her breathing by watching the movement of her chest, rising and falling as she inhaled and exhaled. After a few moments, I picked up Rebecca's right hand and let it drop by itself into her lap. Her arm was very limp. I repeated the same with her left hand and got the same result. Rebecca was now in a somnambulistic rapport. This meant that Rebecca had arrested her conscious mind and her subconscious mind was now wide open. The belief is that the subconscious mind of the individual is the essence of one's self that is indeed the personal soul of the individual given to them at the time of conception. The soul can be impressed upon by one's own personality traits or morals, etc. The soul also has all the knowledge of the universe from the beginning of time until the ending of time by being a part of God himself. That is what I believe to be the link between the individual and God.

The soul is housed within the body and does not dictate to you, but will take dictation from you, be it positive or negative. It has vast amounts of information and keeps storing data as it comes into the mind. The purpose of the soul is to serve you, if you let it do so, as you are the master of your body, mind, and soul.

Here now we were asking the soul of Rebecca to allow her body to join temporarily with another energy or spirit that does not have a physical body. The individual's soul is connected to the physical body by an umbilical cord similar to an embryo fetus. As long as the umbilical cord is connected with the spirit, the spirit remains joined. When the connection is broken, the spirit or soul is free to leave the physical body. The soul or spirit of Rebecca's body can allow a temporary use of the mind and body to an outside spirit by not interfering. When an energy or soul/spirit is lingering nearby and is asked to join with the physical body, the results can be astonishing. Spirits surround us constantly, waiting for an opportunity to communicate with the corporeal world. When I asked Rebecca's soul to move over to the passenger seat of the body and to allow an outside spirit to temporarily occupy the driving seat of the body, it cooperated. The word "temporary" used here is exactly what it means. It is a short use of the time and space of the individual's body.

No outside spirit or soul can possess another body without the consent of the host's soul regardless of whether it is a permanent or temporary possession. The host spirit or soul can evoke the guest soul or spirit from the body at any time. Spirits have to be invited into the host body, and, only

under certain circumstances, can they enter into a body

without the host being aware.

« *V* »

Doris Speaks

Loudly I said, "The body is receptive, the mind is receptive, and the individual soul will be receptive and allow an entry. If an entity is present, make yourself known." I repeated this a few times and suddenly it seemed as if the body was starting to stir and some facial muscle movements were beginning to take place. I then gave instructions to what seemed to be an attempt of an entity. "Whoever you are, you can breathe in unison with the body. You can be in empathy with the body. The body is allowing you to make an entry. That's it; breathe very slowly to adjust with the body."

We watched the head slowly rock back and forth, the arms and hands slightly moved, the fingers clenched into a fist and then the body stretched several times. Her lips were moving as though words were trying to be spoken from her mouth. It appeared that we obviously had an entity struggling to enter and occupy the body of Rebecca. Everyone was watching in awe as the body continued to make erratic movements.

I asked, "Can you hear me clearly?" Rebecca nodded her head up and down indicating an affirmative response. I put my finger to Rebecca's lips to separate them because they were sticking together from dryness. Upon parting the lips, a groaning sound came out and the mouth was moving as if it wanted to speak. I responded and told the entity to take its time and to feel its way through. I explained that it would have the capability of speaking with the vocal chords of the body through the mouth and lips as if it were its own. I started to interrogate the entity.

"Can you identify yourself? Can you tell me your name? Are you male? Are you female? Are you young or old? Are you big or small?"

All these questions and many more were running through my mind. What do I ask first? Would it be friendly or would it be hostile?

The body started to cough as if it were choking. It moved the hands up to the throat as if it were being strangled. It appeared as though the entity was having trouble establishing a rapport with the body of Rebecca.

I yelled, "It's only a memory. It's an affliction of the past memory. The body that is allowing you to make use of it is strong and very healthy. Just relax, take it slow and easy and do not force yourself."

The words suddenly blurted out, "THIS BODY MURDERED ME!"

I pulled her hands down from her neck saying, "Yes, you're murdering the body by eating too much; you're getting fat…"

Rebecca yelled back, "No, you don't understand. This body strangled me! SHE MURDERED ME! She killed me!"

I attempted to calm her down and said, "My name is Raffaele, and I would like to talk to you. Please just listen for a moment and try to relax Rebecca. Breathe deeply and slowly and let yourself adjust to the body. That's it. You can get the words out. I would like to know who you are. Can you tell me your name?"

She again nodded her head affirmatively and slowly let the word Dor…Dor…Doris come forth from her lips. I asked her if she knew where she was, and she shook her head back and forth as if to say no and then she spoke again saying, "I'm not sure. I was there and now I'm here; this is odd." I asked if she was familiar with this general area to which she was allowed to enter. She hesitated, and then said that this area seemed to be familiar to her as though she belonged here or she had been here for a long time.

I asked, "Do you have a middle initial?"

She responded, "Yes, I do. It's A."

I then asked, "Do you have a last name?"

Doris hesitated before responding slowly, "Johnson." She continued to cough as if she were being choked. I told her that feeling would disappear as we continued to talk because it is not an affliction of the body. At this time, I decided to continue with a dialogue with Doris A. Johnson in order to find out more about her and why she came here.

"Doris, now that I know who you are, can you tell me where you lived when you existed in your own body?"

Doris responded, "Waltham."

"Is that Waltham, Massachusetts?" Raffaele asked.

"Yes, it is," Doris replied.

"Where in Waltham?"

"Ash Street, which is near Brown Street."

I then asked, "How old are you?"

She answered, "Almost 50."

"Are you single?"

"Hell, no!"

"Are you married?"

"It's got to be one or the other," Doris sarcastically answered.

"Not necessarily; you could be divorced."

She replied, "No, I've been married twice."

"Do you have any children?" I asked.

"Yes, I have children. Let me see… I have 4 children…2 from each marriage. My first husband died, and I've been divorced for 10 years from hubby #2."

"Open your eyes and look around the room and tell me if you recognize anyone." I instructed her.

Doris opened her eyes and looked around and said, "No, I do not know or recognize anyone here."

To myself I commented, "Wow! We've got someone from our own neighborhood. This will be easy to research later on. I then asked Doris if she was familiar with the body that she was experiencing. As she started to answer, the body began to cough as if it were choking again. I instructed her to breathe a little bit slower. I said, "The body is good and it is strong. It does not have a coughing affliction."

She blurted out, "You're choking me. Stop it!"

I asked her, "Who's choking you? That's only a memory." Then I asked, "Doris, do you know who is talking to you? Do you know where you are?"

Doris replied, "I don't know who the hell you are or where the hell I am."

"How did you get here?" I asked.

"I was standing to the rear of the room next to that fat lady in the middle seat." (The woman in the middle seat was Jeanette Bonina who weighed about 280 pounds).

"How long has it been since you were able to talk like this?" I asked.

Sarcastically she answered, "I'll be damned if I know. Maybe since 1965 or maybe 1967."

"Have you lived in Waltham all your life?"

"Yeah, on Ash Street, Brown Street, and Orange Street. I guess you could say it's been most of my life."

"Did you attend the local school system?"

"Yes, but I quit in the tenth grade."

"Do you have any brothers or sisters?" She didn't answer that question, but again said, "I have three....no four children."

Curiously I asked, "Is Johnson your maiden name or your married name?"

"It's from my second marriage." She answered.

"So, Johnson comes from your second marriage? What is your maiden name?"

Doris replied, "Rose, like the flower."

"What happened to your first marriage?"

"My husband died."

"What was his name?"

"Richard Reade."

"From which marriage were the children born?"

"I had two from each marriage."

"What are their names and ages?"

"Richard is 23; Judy is 22; David is 14; and Sharon is 12."

At this point, Doris became very emotional and started to cry as she spoke of her children and proceeded to tell us that the two young ones lived with her, and she did not know where the two older ones lived. It would appear to me that their ages would be current with the year that this story is being told by the spirit of Doris on March 8, 1984.

I asked her to open her eyes again and to look around the room. In doing so, she looked at the legs of the body from which she was speaking, and then she looked at her left hand. Before she looked at her right hand, I took a full-length mirror and held it in front of her. She could now see the entire existing body sitting in the chair. She looked into the mirror and was puzzled at first. Then she blurted out, "That's me! Yup, that's my body." I thought to myself that she did not see Rebecca's body, but a remembrance of her own body reflecting from the mirror. I removed the mirror and told her to look at her left hand and move it around. She clenched her fist and then relaxed her left hand. She then picked up the right hand and stared at it for a moment.

There was complete silence in the room until Doris got excited and yelled again, "This body murdered me! This body murdered me!"

I tried to calm her down by changing the subject and said, "Yes, the body is overweight, and, yes, it is killing itself."

She looked at me waving the right hand and yelled, "No, No! This body…this one murdered me!"

I put my hand over her eyes to shut them, and, in doing so, I told her to relax, to be calm, and to tell me more about her life. I asked her to describe herself to me as best that she could. She said she was 5'2" tall and weighed about 125 to 130 pounds. She said she had blue eyes and reddish blonde hair. She thought that her age was 34, but after some research a few days later, we discovered she was 48 years old.

She continued and said, "I have a very well-shaped body. I also have a caesarian scar across my stomach and…oh yeah, I am very sexy."

I asked if she could tell me something about where she worked and what she did. She told me she worked near a screw company and thought it had something to do with batteries. It turned out that the screw company was Waltham Screw Company, and the battery company was Perine Battery Company and were both located on Rumford Avenue in Waltham, Massachusetts.

I then asked her if she dated and if she had many men friends. She laughed out loud and said, "Does night follow day?"

I assumed from this statement that she was admitting to having many men friends. I asked her to describe her clothing to me, and she responded, "Can't you see? I'm wearing a multi-colored print dress with the basic color of blue. I have on blue-green high heeled shoes and have my large white pocketbook here with me."

I asked her, "Why are you dressed up?"

She said she had a date and was going out. I asked her where she was planning to go. She told me she was going out for a drink at one of the bars in town and that she was going to meet some of her drinking buddies, but no one in particular. So I asked her who was babysitting for her kids.

She replied, "No one. The two kids are alone."

I was curious which bars she frequented, so I asked her, "To which bar are you going?"

She answered, "It's on Moody Street."

"What is the name of the bar?"

"The 785 Bar, but I don't want to go with him," she added.

Now my curiosity peaked even further, and I had to ask the next question. "With whom don't you want to go?"

"Bruce!" she screeched.

"Easy now. Who is Bruce? Do you know him? What is his last name?"

"I don't know. I just know him as Bruce."

Again I asked, "What is the name of the bar?"

She replied, "It's near the tracks. It's near Tony's."

My questions were not producing the answers as fast as I had hoped. She was being somewhat vague about certain things, but I knew I must continue because I believed there was something here that I couldn't let go. I tried to catch her off guard and quickly asked her, "What year is this?"

Surprisingly to those witnesses in the room, Doris shocked them all by saying, "Why all the questions? Are you a cop or something? It's 1965!" This was two years earlier than her death, and I could not figure out why she flipped out, but I continued to ask questions.

"Does Bruce come here often?"

"On and off when he wants to pick someone up."

"Have you ever gone out with Bruce before?"

"No, and I don't know if I would."

"How long have you worked at Perine Battery Company?"

"About 10 years. I think I started in 1955."

"What about Waltham Screw Company?"

"Oh, that was short lived; maybe one year before I went to Perine Battery."

I decided to pursue another line of questioning, so I asked, "What is your birth date, Doris?"

"I can't remember. I think maybe August. No, maybe September."

"September. What day in September?"

Doris chose not to answer my last question, but she made a statement that had nothing at all to do with my questions.

"I'm at my party."

"Okay, you're at your party. Tell me something about your party."

"We went to Gordon's and then over to the tavern – the Log Cabin on Moody Street."

"You said we; who is we?"

"I went with a girl from work – Anita Juanita, the big fat one, the French broad."

"So the two of you are together and you're going to a party. Where is the party?"

"I don't know, and I don't give a damn. We just want to have a good time and get drunk."

"You just wanted to get drunk? Is that your idea of a good time, Doris?" Then I had to ask, "What month is this, Doris?"

Doris replied, "June? Yeah, it's June; June 1965."

"Do you know what day it is?"

"The 13th…yeah, it's June 13, 1965, and I'm at a party getting drunk."

"How did you dress for the party? Describe yourself to me, Doris."

Doris described how she was dressed. "I let my hair flow long. I'm wearing a blue top that is open at the chest. I am wearing white shoes with open toes, silk stockings, and black pants."

Although I had asked some of these questions before, it was necessary to repeat some of them to see if they matched the previous answers. I wanted to get to the truth, but if they are way off base, the answer can be disregarded; if they are close, it's possible they are true.

I proceeded, "Who is at the party with you?"

"I met a big strong woman. She looked as big as a man. I was frightened by the way she looked at me."

"What is your husband's name?"

"You mean my ex-husband's. Conrad."

"Give me some names. Who is at the party, Doris?"

"Anita Juanita…Who came with me? Larry Davis and Yvonne who lives at the project."

"What is Yvonne's last name?"

"Cormier from Lexington Street. That is her boyfriend over there; the one with the crippled leg. And there's John, Steve, Dick, Frank, Kenny, Bill, Milton and a lot more."

I moved my line of questioning away from the party and on to where she worked. "Doris, who did you work for at Perine Battery?"

She answered, "Marty Scafidi."

"Who else?"

"A little guy; I call him Shorty." She continued, "I'm the inspector and Shorty works on the line with me. It's a hard place to work. Even when the coffee truck comes, they don't want to shut the line down. You have to get your coffee up at the ramp. I can slip you some whiskey out of my thermos if you want it."

Suddenly, Doris repeated over and over again, "You killed me! You killed me!"

I asked, "Who killed you?" Doris became very excited and was extremely uncomfortable whereby she began to move her body in a fidgety manner. She appeared to be talking about two different events in her life. First she was at a party in 1965 having a hell of a time, and then she was recalling a traumatic condition that took her from the physical life back in 1967.

Again I asked her, "Did you go out with Bruce?"

Doris calmed down and said, "Yes! We took a ride out to the Duck Pond."

"What happened at the Duck Pond?"

"We started out just drinking."

"How many drinks did you have? What happened next?"

"Well, you know. We started to kiss and then he put his hand under my blouse and touched my bare breast."

"Okay, continue. What happened next?"

Doris started to cry as she answered. "He then started to take off my clothes. As he pulled at my stocking, I hollered, please don't tear them; they are new; I only wore them once."

"Then what? Did he listen to you?"

"He placed them around my neck so I wouldn't lose them."

"Did he hit you or beat you?"

"No, but he gave me a night of great sex. Then he took me back to the bar."

Many of the witnesses were shocked by her answers. She certainly gave the impressions that she had been around with men friends before.

Doris spoke again and said, "Bruce's father always said Bruce was crazy. All he wanted to do was to have sex. By this time, we got back to the bar, but it was closed. What a night – great drinking, great sex, and I still got home early."

"What kind of car did Bruce drive?" I asked Doris.

"A station wagon."

At this time, the host body is squirming in the big comfortable chair and I asked, "What's the problem, Doris?"

"I'm tired, and I don't want to talk anymore. I want to go back. I don't feel right."

"Okay, but I would like you to stay close by so we may talk again. Is that okay with you?"

"Yeah, okay."

I complied with her request and told her to just float out. I told her to reverse the feelings she had when she came in. All of a sudden, the body jerked and went limp as if it were unconscious.

« *VI* »

The Host Body Regains Composure

Stunned by what just took place, we decided to pursue the line of questioning with the host body. I tapped Rebecca's face gently and called her name. "Rebecca, Rebecca are you okay? Wake up. How do you feel?"

Rebecca claimed that she felt fine and felt as if she had drifted deep into a big dark hole.

I then asked Rebecca, "What do you remember?"

"Nothing, not a damn thing! Was I supposed to?"

"Why are you sweating, Rebecca?"

"I don't know; it's kind of warm in here."

"You're perspiring also. You're hot!"

"I am not hot! I feel warm."

"Tell me again, Rebecca. What do you remember?"

"Going to sleep – like blacking out."

"You felt as though you went to sleep?"

"Yeah, I went down into the hole."

"How did it feel?"

"It felt nice." Rebecca turned to Diane, my associate, and asked, "Did you sleep also, sugar?"

Diane answered, "No, because I was too interested in listening to what you had to say. I find it fascinating. It sounds so true and yet too farfetched to be real."

Being curious, I asked Rebecca if she drank alcohol of any kind. She responded by saying that she never drank any liquor in her entire life. I continued questioning her because I was not sure if she was being truthful and asked if she ever drank Southern Comfort. She laughed and wanted to know if I was kidding with her. I asked her if she ever frequented the local bar rooms.

She shot back quickly, "No, no, never!" She explained that her husband would not allow her to go to bars or any drinking establishments. She said that she only gets to go to the local fraternal clubs and that's only if her girlfriends go with her. She also said that she couldn't stay too long because her husband would unexpectedly walk in and out. She mentioned that she could not drink because she had a bad pancreas. I proceeded to ask if the name Doris had any meaning to her or if she knew anybody by that name. I was trying to get some sort of a reaction or a facial expression that might tell me something different than what I was getting from my direct line of questioning.

She hesitated and hummed as she pondered on the question and then told me she wasn't sure, didn't think so; she really didn't remember anyone by the name of Doris. In an attempt to confuse her, I asked her if she had ever been to Maine. She answered in the affirmative that she had been to Maine several times.

"I go to Old Orchard Beach; sometimes we go to Saco Beach to get a good meal."

"Rebecca, can you tell me your husband's name?"

She questioned why I wanted to know, and I told her there was no particular reason. She then told me his name was James F. Fowler. I proceeded and asked if she knew anyone by the name of Bruce.

"Bruce who?" was her answer.

I asked her if she worked in Waltham.

The answer was affirmative as she said, "Oh yeah! I've worked at the Fernald School for over twenty-nine years." I questioned if she ever worked at Perine Battery Company, and she looked puzzled as she answered that she worked for the entire twenty-nine years at Fernald.

"Tell me, Rebecca, have you ever experienced the feeling as though you were being choked or someone had their hands around your throat in an attempt to choke you?"

She looked at me side-eyed and snapped, "What the hell kind of a question is that? Of course not. I've never had that feeling…never!"

"Rebecca, do you recall anyone talking through your vocal chords or using your body?" She seemed puzzled with the question and wanted to know if something happened or took place while she was sleeping.

"Well, to tell you the truth, someone or something spoke through your vocal chords and said she was murdered in 1965 or 1967."

Rebecca wanted to know if it was a real person or maybe her imagination. She seemed a little uneasy and thought it was weird that she didn't remember what happened.

Confused, she also asked if we actually heard her voice or another voice speaking from her mouth.

One member of the class, Terry Pendleton, commented that she experienced something strange here tonight while sitting in the weight class. She claimed that she had a coughing spell and felt that she was being choked. She also said that she saw an image of a small woman with blonde hair in front of her before she woke up, and when she was listening to and watching Rebecca, it seemed so real...as if it had actually taken place.

No sooner had Terry finished telling her experience, another member, Carol, explained what she also felt while sleeping at the back of the room. She claimed that she heard a noise in the class and opened her eyes. She also said she saw an image of a blonde girl walking back and forth in front of her. She said she was scared and closed her eyes and went back to sleep until the class was instructed to wake up.

As I listened to all of this, I thought something was definitely taking place, and I thought it was up to me to investigate this further. I asked Rebecca for her full name and also asked if she knew a big fat woman by the name of Anita Juanita. Rebecca responded that the name did not ring a bell to her and that she had met many people who were big and fat. I urged Rebecca not to get upset with me because I was asking so many questions, and she in turn told me not to worry about it. I said that I was not worried about it, but I was going to continue with my line of questioning.

"Did you know anyone by the name of Bruce?"

She responded that she knew a Bruce Burns. She then asked, "Was he a heavy set man, and what did he look like because the one I know is a real young kid." I hesitated and instructed my associate to make a notation that this should be researched.

Continuing on, I inquired, "Rebecca, can you tell me when you moved to Waltham, and where you lived before you came here?"

She answered, "I came from Georgia to Waltham and that was over twenty years ago."

This being March 1984, that would mean Rebecca came to Waltham about 1964. I then asked her what her birth date was, and she said it was July 3, 1931. If this is true, Rebecca was about 53 years old. Rebecca interrupted because she was concerned and wanted to know if that girl was going to invade her body again. Puzzled by her statement, I began to wonder if this temporary possession had occurred before tonight's session or if this was the first time. I was concerned because any type of possession without some guidance could lead to danger for the host body.

Rebecca became upset and said, "I don't like her. She drinks, and I don't like going to bar rooms."

At this time, Diane wanted to know what would happen if she took a drink because Rebecca told us she had a bad pancreas. She answered Diane that she would probably pass out, and if left unattended, she could die.

"Rebecca, have you ever worked at Waltham Screw Company on Rumford Avenue?"

She shot back, "I only worked at the Fernald School and that was for 29 years." Although this question had been asked before, it is sometimes necessary to ask again in order to verify the truth.

I asked Rebecca how old she was, and she told me it was none of my business. I agreed with her and explained to her that I was not trying to be nosy. I was only trying to determine her age based on our conversation here tonight.

I continued, "If you came to Waltham 20 years ago, as you claim, that puts you in the years 1964 or 1965, and if you were born in 1931, that would put you at an age of about 53 years old now. I don't think you are 53, however, I think you are about 47 or 48 years old."

Sarcastically she asked, "What difference does it make how old I am anyway?"

I looked at the wall clock and was jolted by the time. It was 1:30 a.m. Where did the time go? Nobody seemed tired, and they wanted to continue this session with Rebecca. I suggested we call it quits for the night, and, as everyone left, you could hear all the speculation of what really took place here tonight.

« *VII* »

Research & Review of Data

The next evening, we listened to the tapes over and over again, attempting to make some sense out of what we heard. There were many contradictory statements, yet the story seemed genuine. Because of all the details presented, it almost sounded as if the story had been rehearsed in order to make us believers. Before we left for the night, I instructed Diane to make some phone inquiries to the Perine Battery Company and the Waltham Screw Company. I wanted to know who the owners, supervisors, and long time employees were at this time and where they might be now. I also instructed her to go to the public library to research the files of old newspapers between the years of 1965 and 1967 to see if a murder took place and if it was reported.

A few days later, I talked to an officer in the local police department who is also a personal friend. I explained to him the events of the last session, and that I believed we may have some information about a possible murder that happened during 1965 and 1967. When I returned to my office, Diane told me she had some luck getting a few telephone numbers of people who supposedly knew Doris. She also showed me headlines on the front page of the 1967 local newspaper from the microfilm files at the public library. They read – *Woman Found Strangled with Silk Stocking Wrapped Around Neck and Body Thrown into Brook*. It further read, "*The body was found partially naked with one breast exposed, her dress wrapped around the armpit and the stocking tied lightly around her neck. Death was by strangulation.*"

It appeared to be a coincidence that the dates, body gender, and type of murder, etc. all fit with our information. However, I do not believe in coincidences. I believe in syncrosity, wherein all things move and if they are to join with other things by meshing, they then would be synchronized. Henceforth, synchrosity is a form of blending, whereas all things happen for a reason or purpose.

Once again, Diane and I reviewed the cassette tapes of the session with Rebecca very carefully. We matched events and information that were closely related, and we also noted the areas that were way off base. I believed that if Rebecca was trying to pull a scam, it would have been necessary for her to have a photographic memory, for more than 70% of the details were very near on target. It could be possible that she knew about the murder or had heard about the murder in conversation. This was all mind-boggling, so much so that we decided to further investigate and do extensive research to the maximum. The following day I received a copy of the police case file that I requested from my friend in the homicide division. The information read as follows:

"Murder of Doris A. Johnson, age 47, of 25 Ash Street, Waltham, Massachusetts. Date of birth September 2, 1917. Found dead on Wednesday morning, August 16, 1967. Doris was seen in front of her house on Tuesday, 7:30 P.M. by her neighbor, Ms. Anita White, while waiting for her date. Ms. Anita White said that Doris was wearing a multi-colored print dress, predominantly blue, with a new pair of green high-heeled patent leather shoes. Doris...maiden name is Johnson. She was described as being 5'2" tall and weighed in at about 135-140 pounds. She had reddish-brown hair and the colors of her eyes were blue. Her abdomen had a scar from Caesarean birth. She was married to Richard Reade and had two children with him. They had a son, Richard, Jr., about 28 years old, and a daughter, Judy, about 22 years old. Richard Reade is deceased. Doris then married Conrad Johnson and has been separated for about ten years. She had two children with him also. There was David, who was about 14 years

old and a daughter, Sharon, who was about 12 years old. Her ex-husband is living is New Hampshire. She was employed as a factory worker for the Waltham Screw Company on Woerd Avenue and was formerly employed by Perine Battery Company on the same street. According to eye witnesses, the victim, Doris, came in to the Log Cabin alone on Tuesday night about 8:30 p.m. She sat at the bar, according to the owner, Frank Carminiti, and watched the entire ball game on television. Frank said Doris had one bottle of beer and left the Log Cabin just a little after midnight. She had some conversation at the bar with a customer, Leroy Manning. Leroy Manning left the tavern alone about 12:30 a.m. He does not have a car. Information from her daughter revealed that Doris told her she had a date with someone named Walter that night. It was determined to be Walter Norton of Newton, age 31 years old, and he owned a 1962 blue Ford Thunderbird. A few houses from Doris's house, a neighbor had come home *about 11:30 p.m. He stated that about 1:00 a.m. he was awakened by a woman's voice hollering, "Stop! Don't do that! It hurts!"*

He looked out the window and saw a big black Cadillac. He saw a small woman and a rather large man on the hood of the car engaging in sexual activity. He said he couldn't identify them. Another male friend, 36 years old, was interviewed and said he knew Doris intimately for over five years. He also said she was seeing some big time contractor named Dick Freni. Dick was 32 years old and owned a successful service station in the general area where the body was found. Doris was employed on a part-time basis for Freni as a bookkeeper. Freni is a married man and owned a 1962 Oldsmobile station wagon. Freni is also seeing a married woman named Ruth from Ashland. His favorite hangout is the Auburndale Cafe', which is not too far from the site where the body was found. It seemed that Freni was in New Hampshire the week the murder took place. Mrs. Freni said her husband left New Hampshire on Tuesday afternoon, August 15, 1967, and did not return to New Hampshire.

He opened the service station early Wednesday morning because his assistant came in late. Doris's husband, Conrad Johnson, who is 54 years old, said he and his girlfriend saw Doris outside of her house at 5:30 p.m. on Thursday, August 15. They just happened to drive by her street. Doris's body was found by an employee of the paper mill about 7:30 a.m. on Wednesday morning, August 16, 1967. In addition to her dress, she was also wearing a white half slip and a black bra. None of the clothes were ripped or torn. The dress was wrapped up around her armpit. Her left breast was completely exposed. She was strangled with her own nylon stocking that was typically tied around her throat. Although she was in water, her head was facing up so that death was not by drowning, but by asphyxiation. Her blood alcohol analysis showed a 0.10% alcohol content.

After digesting what I had just read, it was clearly evident that this rather small woman at the age of 47 was dating and having sex with a half dozen men much younger than her age by some 15-17 years. Any one of them could have been suspected of killing her. They were all drinking buddies to some extent. They all frequented the same bars and cafes. They all seemed to know each other very well. Assuming all of this is true, how does Rebecca fit into this scenario? She claimed she did not drink; therefore, she would have no reason to hang out in bar rooms. However, somehow their paths crossed, if only for a brief time.

« *VIII* »

A Blast from the Past

It seemed as if there was too much detail for Rebecca to memorize, so therefore did we actually have the spirit of Doris speaking through the body of Rebecca? Scanning the names of the people who were identified by Rebecca as working at Perine Battery and Waltham Screw Company, I recognized several of them. I made it a point to call one of the people listed. His name was Joe Rigoli who is also a friend of mine from the local fraternal club, "The Loyal Order of Moose." During our conversation, he mentioned that he knew of the girl who was murdered, and he could lead me to a few other people such as the foreman and supervisors of the plants. Joe told me that Perine Battery Company had burned down and most of the employees were scattered around the other cities and towns. Joe gave me a good lead to a battery company in Framingham, which led me to Steve Tardy who, at one time, was the foreman at Perine Battery Company. I searched out the telephone number and put a call to the battery company in Framingham and asked for Steve Tardy. I asked Steve if he remembered a girl by the name of Doris Johnson who worked at the plant with him.

Steve said he recognized the name and asked if she was the girl they found strangled. I said. "Yes, the same one."

He proceeded to tell me that he had someone there with him who dated and was intimate with Doris. I was excited with this news and asked if he could give me his name and if it was possible for me to talk to him. He told me to wait a minute and he would dial his section for me. Steve picked up the intercom phone and said loud and clear, "Hey, Shorty, there is someone who would like to talk with you!"

When I heard the name Shorty, I thought to myself that this must be a nickname and could easily be traced. When Shorty got on the phone, I asked if I could set up a lunch date with him, Steve, my associate and me.

I made reservations for the next day at one of the restaurants in Framingham. Diane and I met with them, and after introductions we ordered some food and beverage. While waiting for our orders, I decided to open up with a question to both of them.

"Do you guys believe in ghosts?" You could have heard a pin drop with a loud bang. They looked at each other, then at Diane and me.

Shorty said, "Are you kidding? This is not Halloween."

I assured them that we were not kidding around and that we came upon an incredible condition in reference to the woman they both knew. "It seems," I continued, "she has invaded a host body and is speaking to us, revealing many personal stories. Some were about both of you."

Both Steve and Shorty were amazed and Shorty said, "That's too heavy for me. It scares the crap out of me."

Shorty proceeded to tell us that he dated Doris many times and had sex with her almost as many times as he had dated her. He also volunteered the information that many of the other guys at the shop had sex with her as well and claimed that after one drink she became very promiscuous and acted like a nymphomaniac.

I asked Shorty if there was anything unusual about Doris, such as her style of dress, jewelry, handbags, etc. Shorty pondered a moment and said, "Yeah. There was something very strange about her. Although she liked to have sex, she always seemed to wear a sterling silver religious thing around her neck. I found that kind of strange."

"Wouldn't you guys like to come to our next session to meet Doris?"

Steve responded, "No way! She may reveal more of what we probably forgot, and we don't need that problem."

I reached into my briefcase and pulled out some Polaroid pictures. I took these pictures while Rebecca was drifting into a deep trance in one of our sessions. I showed the pictures to both Steve and Shorty, and they both agreed that neither one of them had seen nor recognized this huge woman. I told them that she was the host body for Doris, and Doris seems to occupy this body and communicates with us. I inquired if they had any objection if I took a Polaroid picture of each of them, so I could bring the pictures back to my office. They answered in the affirmative. I invited Steve and Shorty to come to the next session as surprise guests and confront Doris. I proceeded to explain that this could get a great reaction. They thought it would be a good idea, but it was not their cup of tea, and it would bother them because they did not understand what was happening.

I requested from them a detailed explanation of some of the terminology or modus operandi of battery work. This would help us to ask intelligent questions about how batteries are developed. They explained that separators go into the battery and "tiegle burning" is the process of burning the plates together by lead straps. "Finish line" is the process of placing the units into the final cases.

Before we realized it, the hour-long lunch was over. Diane and I thanked them for their time. I picked up the tab for lunch, and we parted our ways. We thought the meeting was very successful, as it provided us with insight and knowledge into Doris's life prior to her death. Diane took notes that we reviewed when we arrived back at the office. When we finally went over the notes a second time, we had some questions on a few things. We were sure that we had gathered enough material in that one short week so that at the next session we would be prepared so as not to be tripped up by Rebecca, alias Doris. We agreed on a plan to place the Polaroid pictures I took of Steve and Shorty on the coffee table together with several other photos of males for everyone to see.

« IX »

The Victim Returns

As we all know, men and women alike are curious creatures, so as expected, when everyone came in to the reception area, one by one they picked up the pictures to look at them. We were more concerned with Rebecca's reaction when she looked at the pictures. She went through all twelve photos and asked what they were all about without blinking an eye. She was unaware that we were studying her actions and reactions. After a reasonable amount of time, we were convinced that she did not recognize anyone in the pictures, for if she did, then she was a good actress and kept it all well hidden. We went on with the weight class as usual and finally the hour had come to get on with the next session. Everyone seemed excited and anxious to get started.

I proceeded as I usually do when working with a subject. It wasn't too long before we had a rapport with an entity that entered the body of Rebecca, who, at this time, was experiencing a deep sleep. As expected, the voice came through Rebecca's vocal chords, and the entrance into the host body was the same choking condition that was evident at the last session. It appeared to us that whatever the entity had experienced just before or during death seemed to be the same feeling all over again as if it were the first time upon each entry.

The entity struggled to speak as if being choked, "The stocking; it's wrapped around my throat. I can't breathe; I'm too weak; I'm drunk; I can't move; the water is cold; I'm too drunk to swim."

Assuming these words were being spoken by Doris Johnson, I immediately called her by name and said, "Drift back, Doris, drift back. Easy; go back before the water; before the choking. Where are you, Doris?" It appeared that the host body was uncomfortable accepting this possession, but had no choice but to allow it to continue.

Calmly, Doris answered, "I'm at someone's house trying to get a bottle of alcohol."

I asked Doris if she could identify the house or its location, if she knew the people who lived there, and how long they had been there. Doris replied that the house was on Crescent Street and didn't seem to know the occupants of the house. She thought the guy she was with knew them well, and they were only there long enough to get a bottle. She went on to say that she didn't get out of the car.

"Can you tell me what happened after you got the bottle?"

"It's hard for me to remember. I've been drinking all night. I feel drunk."

"How late is it, Doris?"

"Maybe 12:00 or 12:30. I don't know."

"Tell me, Doris, do you ever think about anything else besides drinking and having sex?"

"Sometimes I think about my kids. Where are they now? I don't think they want to know me or remember me anymore."

"Okay, Doris, relax a bit more and listen very carefully. I am going to want you to open your eyes in a little while. Just as you are using the body's vocal chords to let your voice be heard, you can see through the body's eyes and feel with the arms, hands, and feet. Now very slowly, move the eyelids to open the eyes. That's it, you're doing just fine. Now look at me. Turn your head to look at me. Can you see me?"

Doris followed my instructions and when her eyes were opened, she muttered, "I don't know you. Who are you?"

"I am Raffaele, and I am going to introduce you to everyone who is here tonight. Ladies and gentlemen, this is Doris. Doris, from your left to right is Terry, Joan, Steve, Millie, Marcia, Joey, Susan, Jeannette, Dianne, Norma, Josie, Janet, Janice, James, and my associate Diane."

"Why are all these people here?" Doris sniped.

"They are interested in your story, Doris. They want to know what happened to you."

"I was killed! That is what happened to me." Doris shouted.

"How do you feel in the body in which you have occupied recently?"

"It's big, much bigger than my own."

She pulled the blouse from her chest to look down. She declared, "Oh yeah, she has bigger breasts than I had. I could have used these. Boy, the guys sure would have loved these!"

As Doris was adjusting herself to the body, I noticed her looking more and more at Steve and Joey, the male observers in the group. They were young men in their mid to late twenties. As Doris indicated many times while in session, she liked men who were much younger than herself. The setting seemed to fit her. I told her to sit still for a few moments because I wanted to take a picture of her with my Polaroid camera. I focused in on the body and pushed the button. Off went the flash!

Stunned she shouted, "You blinded me! I can't see! The lights hurt my eyes!"

After a few seconds, she quieted down, and I placed the picture in her hands and told her to observe the developing process. She was amazed to see the picture come alive before her eyes.

When it was completed, she stared and stared and screeched, "That's not me!" I agreed with her and told her that it was someone else's body that she was using temporarily. I attempted to divert her attention away from the host body and picked up the other dozen pictures that were displayed downstairs. I instructed Doris to look closely at these photographs. We all waited anxiously for her reaction, if any, when she saw Shorty.

As she was looking at the pictures, one by one, she came to Steve Tardy. She stared at it and said, "This guy looks familiar." She proceeded to look at the next one which was Shorty. This triggered a heightened excitement to the extent where she now seemed happy and called out his name several times.

"I haven't seen Shorty since we worked together at Perine Battery. Where did you get his picture? He's a little balder than he was, but he's the same old Shorty. Boy, he was a great lover."

We were all taken aback by her reaction to Shorty's picture because when Rebecca came in earlier in the evening and looked at these pictures, there was no reaction at all, although we had hoped for this very condition from both Rebecca and Doris. I still kept an open mind and questioned the fact of whether Rebecca did recognize the pictures and kept her reaction hidden, and I wondered if Doris had overreacted. I would have to say in all of my experience in working with people in this particular area, I have to believe that Rebecca did not know nor did she recognize Shorty's picture based on the fact that she overlooked Steve Tardy's picture who was the person in charge of hiring and firing at the plant.

Doris was hesitant and did not discard or overlook the fact that Steve Tardy's picture looked very familiar. Again, much to our surprise, Doris asked, "Can you bring Shorty here to me? I want to see him in person. I want to feel him, and I'd love to have sex with him again."

I explained that I would try to have him here at the next session. Wow! Our imaginations were running wild! Suppose he agreed to come and she embraced him with this huge body. It might kill him. What if she tried to attack him with such lust? She could hurt him. She could be successful because Shorty is only five feet tall, and this female body that Doris is using is over six feet. Shorty looked as though he weighed 150 pounds, and Rebecca's body looked over 200 pounds. As I said, our imaginations were running wild.

I took the pictures from Doris and said, "Let's continue with our talk." Doris started to rub Rebecca's hands together and was mumbling as she rubbed the missing thumb area. In a rage, she blurted out, "She murdered me!

She murdered me!" I attempted to calm her down for I had more questions.

I asked if she knew a place called the "105."

Still mumbling to herself, she abruptly replied, "No, no. I don't know that place."

"Did you ever frequent the Log Cabin?"

"Oh yes, I knew the waitress there."

"Who? What is her name?"

"It's Yvonne. Yvonne Cormier."

"How about the bartender?"

"He's an old man. I never got to know him."

This statement seemed to fit Doris's pattern because she kept the company of men who were much younger than her, and she admitted the bartender was an old man. I thought I could catch her on the next question when I asked Doris if she could recall the location of the Log Cabin and if she knew what was directly across the street.

She shot right back with, "Gordon's, Gordon's liquor store was across the street, but I don't know if it's still there." She was right. There was a liquor store across the street in those days.

Diane asked, "It seems that you went out drinking every night and left your children home alone. Is this true?"

Defensively, Doris boasted, "I work hard every day. I'm entitled to go out at night. They are 12 and 14 years old. They are old enough to stay home alone. I get up every morning at 5:00 a.m., and I go to work. So what if I drink every night? I work very hard for my money."

"How much money do you earn per week?" asked Raffaele.

"If we produce one hundred and fifteen batteries, I can earn over $100 a week. If we can do an extra fifteen a day, we get an extra $75 a week. We're piece workers. I remember Mike being very sick; you know he's here with me now."

"What do you mean he's here with you now?"

"He passed on and came here about six or seven years ago."

"Doris, do you know what year this is?"

"No, why did something happen that I should know?"

"This is the year of 1984, which is about seventeen years since you were found dead, murdered!"

"My kids! My kids! They must be all grown up."

"That is correct; they are all seventeen years older. What took you so long to approach us? I have been experimenting in this area for a long time. You could have communicated at any given time. Why now and not sooner?"

"I had to wait for her! I knew she was coming. I had to wait. It had to be her! I have to get even!"

Raffaele thought for a moment and wondered to whom she was referring. Why did she have to get even? As we got deeper into this, more questions came to mind.

"How long have you been here? How long have you been with us?"

"It's been over five years. I've been watching. Who do you think led the bitch here to you, Santa Claus? I led her here. I had to wait. It took five years to reach this point. Now I have her where I want her. Now it is my turn! We'll see."

This sounded as if she was seeking revenge against Rebecca. Was this really Doris's spirit speaking through Rebecca's body or was Rebecca involved in the alleged murder? If so, and after all this time, was the guilt too heavy to bear and was it now showing itself from Rebecca's subconscious mind?

I asked Doris, "What do you mean it's your turn?"

Doris responded, "You'll see when I do it."

"You said that you have been hanging around here for five years. Where did you hang out?"

"In the back of the room at the last row. I had fun teasing your clients as they drifted out. I would touch them and sometimes appear in flashes to them," Doris remarked.

"You mentioned the name Mike. Does Mike come from Waltham?"

"Sure as hell does."

"Where did he live?"

"Here off Hamlin Street. Didn't you go to the big wedding?"

Not sure what Doris was alluding to, Raffaele said no and then asked, "Doris, where did you live before you got married?"

"Orange Street, then Brown Street, and now Ash Street which is right around the corner from here."

"What were your father's and mother's names?"

Bitterly, Doris declared, "Edith and Charles. I don't want to talk about my father. Forget about him; he forgot about me."

"Was your father a drinker?" Diane questioned.

"Of course he is. Everybody drinks."

To reaffirm in an attempt to catch Doris off guard, Diane posed a similar question. "What is across from Gordon's Liquors? What is across the street from there?"

Upset by the repeated question, Doris yelled out loud, "What the hell are you doing? Are you trying to play games with me? I told you before, it's the Log Cabin."

Raffaele then interjected and asked, "What else is up on Moody Street?"

"You mean the funeral parlor and a house? Wait! Wait! There was another bar called Hagin's, Hagin's. Also there is Como's. Juanita and I went in there all the time."

Diane commented to Doris, "You seem to know where all the bars are located."

Doris shot back, "Damn right! We also go to Casella's and The 785 Club."

Diane asked, "So you're covering all the bars in the area. What about Fritz's and Wanda's?"

"Oh yeah." Doris remembered. "And what about Patrick's in Watertown?"

Raffaele cut in and asked Doris, "What school did you attend?"

Trying to recall, Doris slowly replied, "New...New....Newhall School."

"Did you attend the Whittemore School?"

"No, my kids did."

Raffaele then asked, "Can you give me more names of people you knew or hung out with when you were at the Log Cabin?"

"There was a young person, a Larry Davis, from Robbins Street, also another guy named Billy. A lot of guys just breeze in and out, especially from up the street; the ones with the motorcycles."

"Rebecca, how do you feel?"

"My name is not Rebecca, it's Doris!"

"Okay, I do that once in a while just to double check."

"Don't ever call me Rebecca. My name is Doris and don't you ever forget it." she warned.

It seems that Doris became very upset when I purposely called her Rebecca. This would indicate that there was a very strong resentment towards Rebecca, and it could also be the beginning of her action in getting this so-called revenge…to get even.

"Doris, can you see everything down here when you go back up there, wherever it is you go?"

"I see everything and everyone, no matter where they are or what they are doing."

She continued to explain and laughed, "even if they're having sex. Sometimes I have fun by pinching them. Boy, do they jump! They don't know where it's coming from or by whom."

It was getting very late, so Raffaele said, "Okay, that should be enough for tonight. I'm going to ask you to leave until we meet the next time."

Sarcastically, Doris came back with, "Suppose, I don't want to leave?"

"Why would you not want to leave?"

"Maybe I want to control this body; get even for what she did to me."

"What has this body done to you? Why do you keep saying that you want to get even? Why is revenge so important? It must have been terrible."

"She murdered me! She murdered me!"

"You keep mumbling that, and yet there were seven or eight guys who could have just as easily murdered you."

"The light is coming. It is hurting my eyes. I'll go."

"Okay, Doris, just slip out in reverse of the way you came into the body."

"Don't worry; I can slip in and out any time and in any place of my choosing. I'll get even with her, that's for sure." threatened Doris.

As Doris slipped out, Rebecca's body remained limp and asleep. As usual, I tapped her on her cheek and asked if she could hear me. As her eyes started to open, I asked her how she felt, and if she could remember anything that took place. Rebecca said she had the most wonderful, relaxed sleep that she experienced in a very long time, and she couldn't remember anything that took place or any conversation. It was nothing more than a very deep, relaxing sleep.

This became more amazing because on one side we have a physical body that seems to have an attraction to a deceased body's entity, and on the other side it seems we have a very strong energy or soul who wants to possess Rebecca's body and take revenge on the body. I asked all who were there as witnesses if they had any questions, and, if they did, I instructed them to write them down and present them at the next session. They all agreed because there were too many questions to be answered. For instance, how could Rebecca know so many names and places? If Doris were a spirit, how could she temporarily possess the body of Rebecca? Did Doris want Rebecca's body to absorb alcohol, knowing full well that if Rebecca consumed alcohol, it could kill her. Was this the revenge? Remember, Rebecca has a bad pancreas. It seems Doris is obsessed with the fact that Rebecca murdered her. There didn't seem to be a reason or motive for Rebecca to murder Doris. We know by the admission of the spirit that Doris was a very promiscuous woman. She enjoyed sex to no ends and enjoyed drinking every night. It also seemed that she enjoyed being with men who were much younger than herself. Yet, she seemed to be a conscientious and dependable worker at the plant.

As all of this was being discussed, I noticed that Rebecca was sort of daydreaming in the chair. I hollered at her a few times in an attempt to bring her forward to a wakening state. Was this Doris's spirit playing games, attempting to influence the body by possessing her? Did she mean it when she said that she could slip in and out of the body at will any time? This didn't seem right. In all my past experience, the guest spirit never attempted to override the host's body or mind. Was Doris attempting to take on

Rebecca's personalities and then occupy the body for her own purpose?

You heard her say, "Boy, what large breasts this body has! I bet the guys would love this." Could she carry over a personality of such lurid sex that she could influence the body when I was not present? I asked the powers above for protection of all involved whether they be participants or witnesses. I now had another concern. I would have to monitor Rebecca and this meant keeping in close touch to see if anything out of the ordinary was going to take place. I reaffirmed my command and ordered Rebecca to open her eyes. It took longer than usual, but after a few minutes, she was fully awake.

Bewildered, the class observers all agreed that this session was fascinating and intriguing, but many questions remained unanswered. We anxiously looked forward to the next session. I had some questions pertaining to the strength of the spirit possession that was intensifying over time. Before Rebecca left the office this night, I asked her to call me a few times during the week. I didn't want to frighten her with my reasoning, so I simply told her that I would like to hear from her if she had the time. She responded that she would make the time to talk to me.

« *X* »

Doris Begins Her Revenge

One morning at approximately 2:00 a.m. while working late at my office, the phone rang. The voice on the other end said, "I told you I could get to her."

It was Doris and I angrily asked, "What the hell are you doing? You were not asked to make an appearance."

She vowed, "I'm just starting to get even. This body can't hold her booze."

I yelled at Doris and told her to leave and let me talk to Rebecca.

"Sure, you can talk to her. She's drunk and sitting on the floor with some half-empty bottles around her. I took her around town tonight. We went to Boston, Malden, and

Watertown. We spent lots of her money, and then I led her back home."

At that moment, the voice changed back to Rebecca, and, somewhat intoxicated, Rebecca slurred her words and asked, "With whom am I talking?"

I told her it was Raffaele.

"Boy," she said, "did Doris make a mess out of me tonight. I'm drunk and I'm not supposed to drink."

I could hear the clinking of bottles as if someone was hitting them together. I was very firm and told Rebecca. "You are not to listen to Doris unless I am in your presence."

Rebecca said, "I can handle her. I like the way she feels."

Again I told Rebecca to get up and pour the alcohol down the sink and not to drink anymore. I made her promise me to do exactly what I told her.

Rebecca said, "Raffaele, Doris won't hurt me. I have a good feeling for her. I like her. She could be good for me or even good to me. I need her."

Again I yelled through the phone, "You do not need Doris, and get hold of yourself. You always told me you were a strong-minded woman, so show me that you are that woman. Reject Doris now, do it!" She hung up the phone, and I did not hear from her until the next session.

« *XI* »

The Plot Thickens

The evening commenced as usual. First we had the weight class and then the special group followed to investigate unknown phenomena, which at the time, was the case of Doris and Rebecca. Rebecca responded rather quickly on this night. There was no hesitation at all. She took one deep breath, closed her eyes, and off she went into a deep sleep.

Immediately, Doris's voice came in loud and clear and her opening statement was, "The lights are too bright. Dim them down a bit."

Upon dimming the lights, she opened her eyes wide and said hello to everyone in such a way that she gave the impression this was her own body, and it was very natural. I opened the questioning by asking if she remembered everything about the last meeting, and she confirmed that she remembered everything and that she does not forget anything.

I continued my questioning and asked, "What happened to you when you left here last week, Doris?"

"Nothing happened. It was the same dull thing."

"Like what?" I asked. "What did you do? Where did you go?"

I followed the body home."

"Why?"

"To see if I could reach her without your help."

"And did you?" Were you successful?"

"No, I wasn't."

I knew this was not true, and I objected strongly, so I lashed out at her saying, "Doris, you're lying! You know damn well you reached her!"

"I did not," Doris shouted.

"Did you not call me during the week and tell me that you did get to her?"

"No, that was her. Rebecca called you, not me. I don't know your number, but she does."

"Then why did you communicate with me? You could have left when the phone rang. But NO, you had to prove that you had control and could do what you set out to accomplish."

"So what! You can't blame me for wanting revenge. You know what she did to me. You'll see. I'll tell you when I'm ready."

Diane was sitting by Rebecca's body taking notes as she usually does, and suddenly she changed the line of questioning. "Doris, tell me about your friend, Juanita."

"She's my drinking buddy. Why do you ask? I've known her for a long time."

"Describe her to me."

"She has big thighs and big breasts; she's a big girl."

"Did she work with you?"

"I inspected and she was on production. We had to get out 1500 batteries a day."

"That's a lot of batteries. How much did you say you made a week?"

"One hundred dollars."

Raffaele then took over the questioning and asked, "What is your favorite color?"

"Blue…I love the color blue. It matches my eyes."

"What were you wearing the night you went to the pond?"

"Blue print; a full dress—it looked like a blouse and skirt, but it was a full dress."

"What about your undergarments?"

"Boy, you're persistently nosy. Next you'll want to sleep with me just like all the other guys did."

"No, no Doris, I'm just trying to see where the truth lies. I know what color your undergarments were. I read the police records."

"I wore a white slip, black bra, black sexy panties and nylon stockings, sort of black lace."

"What about your shoes? What kind of shoes were you wearing? Were they sneakers, boots, or high heels?"

"High heels. They were blue like my eyes but sort of green. I also had my pearl-white pocketbook with very little in it."

"Doris, did you ever go out with a fellow named George?"

"Which one? George Rowley? I also went out with Harry and another George and Larry. They were all good drinking buddies, and they all lusted after my body. Believe me; I had no problems in that department."

"Did you know someone named Mirabito?"

"I probably did."

"In other words, you were friendly to anyone who wanted to have sex with you?"

"Nothing wrong with that. I always say make love not war; lots of love; drunk in love."

"Did you wear glasses?"

"Yes, with big rims. They were pointed glasses."

"Did you ever wear boots?"

"Short ones, if I had to, but Shorty liked my…………."

Before she had a chance to finish, I interjected, "Red ones?"

"Yes, red ones. How did you know?"

"Shorty told me there was something special about you when you wore the red ones. It made you look good, and you were much more in the mood for sex, like a wild cat. Who did you say was your big boss?"

"Marty Scafidi."

"Who was over Marty?"

"Someone upstairs. I believe it was Steve Tardy."

"Did you know Joe Rigoli?"

"I knew two people named Rigoli."

"Did your drinking interfere with your work?"

"No. I was always sober when I worked."

"What is the best present that anyone could ever give you, Doris?"

"Booze, lots of booze."

"How old were you when you started drinking?"

"I was twelve years old, and boy, what a buzz I put on."

"How about your mother and father? Did they have a drinking problem?"

"Heavily; they were always drinking; that's how I learned."

"What happened between you and your first husband?"

"I left him. He didn't approve of my lifestyle."

"Why? Did he hurt you?"

"No, he was not a good drinking buddy, and he was much older than me. Raffaele, you promised me a drink. Where is it?"

In an attempt to stall Doris from having a drink, I continued to badger her with questions. After all, we knew the host body had a bad pancreas. "Tell me more about Bruce. Do you want him to continue doing to others what he did to you?"

"I don't remember. I don't know. There's something about a hand...the hand. Where is my drink?"

Facetiously I said, "You drank it! It was a Southern Comfort. You also drank the bourbon I had here."

"I don't remember drinking anything. Are you sure?"

"It's getting late, and you have had a lot of confusing questions asked of you tonight. You're not even sure if you are telling the truth or if everything you've said could be a lie. You're just not sure anymore."

"I don't lie. I did not lie. Everything I told you is the truth. I have no need to lie."

"You told me you were born near the Frye River in Maine, but you were born in Worcester, Massachusetts. Why did you lie to me about that?"

"I'm not lying to you. Sometimes it's hard to remember. It's been so long, and I've wanted to get even for so long I sometimes get my answers mixed up and then you think I'm lying. I'm not lying to you. I just want to get even. I want revenge, and I'm going to get it and nobody better get in my way to try and stop me. I will get my revenge; only then will I go back where I came from."

"Can you tell me where it is you came from?"

"Not until it's all over between her and me."

"Doris, where did you go for coffee breaks at work? Did the company have a coffee machine?"

"No, we had a catering truck that came around. We called it the coffee truck."

"Do you remember who owned the coffee truck?"

"Yes, it was Charlie Manero; he was a young kid."

"What's the problem, Doris? You're squinting your eyes."

"I just remembered the black man who worked with us. His name was Dick Herbert. I see him here for coffee every day. I think he likes me."

"Did you ever go drinking with Dick Herbert?"

"He's not the first man I was with. As long as they like to drink and love sex, that is all I care about. Nothing else means anything."

"Everyone I talk to seems to think that you are a nice girl who is always dressed neatly."

"I don't hurt anyone or cause any trouble. I just like booze and sex."

"What about your neighbor, Ms. Anita White? She said she saw you waiting for your date Tuesday night on August 15, 1967."

"I never spoke to her. She lives at #10 or #12. I'm sure she has seen me go out many times. We only live a few houses apart from each other."

"Describe your friend Bruce again."

"He's decent looking with a round face and a scar on his cheek. He's a little on the fat side. He's also a very rough lover; like an animal."

"Doris, I think we will call it quits for tonight. I have to go over a lot of notes from this session, and I need some time to search out more of these names and places you gave to me. It seems the more I talk to you, the more men friends you reveal. It could have been any one of them, especially if you refused to have sex with them. They could have gotten upset and mad, and then in a fit of rage strangled you. It could be a possibility."

Doris seemed bewildered at what I just said and wasn't quite sure of what I was saying was a logical way of looking at the situation because she blurted out, "No. no. There's something about the hand. It will come to me, but I'll go if you say so. I can always influence Rebecca at any time."

Being upset by her remarks, I flatly stated vehemently, "Doris, you are not to do that! I mean it! Do you understand me?"

"What are you going to do about it? If she lets me in, I'll influence her to no ends."

At this time, the body went limp and Rebecca's eyes opened. She looked around and wanted to know what had happened. She asked if she could hear the tapes that recorded the sessions and then she changed her mind and did not want to hear them. I asked Rebecca to come to my office within a couple of days so we could talk.

When everyone left for the evening, my associate, Diane, asked me why I wanted to have a talk with Rebecca. I told her that I felt it was important that Rebecca tell me a lot more about herself than what we already knew. I also said that I wanted to check into her background because I had a feeling that something did not add up.

« *XII* »

Life on the Plantation

During the middle of the following week, Rebecca came to my office unexpectedly, just as she always did.

Her opening statement was, "You wanted to talk to me. So let's talk. Let's find out what it is that you want to know about me."

Apparently, she was ready to tell all because she went on and on. I listened intently as she began the story of her life.

"I was born in Augusta, Georgia on July 3, 1937. I traveled a lot. I came to Waltham about 1965 with my Cousin Caroline. She looks a lot like me and sometimes people think we are twins. What fun we had confusing people. I'm married and have two children – a son and a daughter. I have one of each and none of the other kind. My father is a real southerner. I mean real Southern. You know, we had a lot of blacks on our plantation. Momma was timid, but she always got what she wanted."

I interrupted and said, "Slow down a bit. Let's go back to your childhood. You mention the words plantation, blacks, real Southerner. Can you tell me what you remember as a little girl?"

"I can remember having black maids and servants in my Daddy's house. My Daddy was mean to all the black men. He would whip them for no reason. I even saw him kill some."

"How did you feel about that when you saw it happen?"

"Well, they deserved it."

"What do you mean they deserved it? No one deserves to be killed."

"Whatever my Daddy wanted, he got it, and if they got him mad enough, he would kill them."

"That's wrong, Rebecca. Nobody has the right to kill anyone no matter how mad they get you."

"I saw one time when a black boy stole something from another black boy. He had the boy stuffed into a big pipe, something like a cesspool pipe in the ground, and put the cover back on. The boy couldn't come out so he drowned and Daddy left him in there. I saw Daddy hang a black boy because he answered him back. You know, after a while, it got to be sort of an exciting thrill to see it happen. After all, we owned them…all of them."

"How did you feel about this as you got older?"

"I sort of got mixed up in the head about it. As a young kid, I would play with the black kids, and as I grew older, they did not want to play with me. They were afraid of me. Everyone said I had my Daddy's blood, and it would only be a matter of time before I would kill someone. I used to beat the black kids with my Daddy's whip. I got good with the whip."

"Did you feel superior? Did you feel stronger? Did you feel more important because you could inflict pain and hurt on someone else?"

"I am superior! I am a stronger woman! See my muscles. Look at the size of me – I'm a big woman! Of course, it made me important and that felt good. I was in command."

"Didn't you ever stop to think or realize that what you felt or what you were doing was wrong, and maybe some day you would have to account for all of your actions on how you treated the servants or people who were less fortunate than you?"

"Action Jackson! Baloney! My Daddy told me the strong always win."

"Did your Daddy ever spank you or beat you?"

"No way! What I wanted, I got. I was Daddy's little girl. Let me tell you about an incident when I was 17 years old. I would sneak out after dark and hide in the bushes down by the swimming hole, and I quietly watched the servants swimming naked in the pond. Many times I would watch them having sex, and it stirred up an excitement that was different from anything I had ever felt. I had sex with a young man from the other plantation, but what I felt was nothing in comparison to this. One night I spotted a young servant about eighteen years old. Wow! Was he well endowed! My body tingled, and I knew I had to be with him. I had to figure out a way so that we could be together alone. I later found out that his name was Henry, and he was the stud of the young girls on the plantation."

She continued. "Then one day I was alone in the big house. Everyone had gone out, and I did not want to go. It was early afternoon, and it was very hot and humid. Henry

113

had come up to the big house to do some cleaning around the grounds. Since it was so hot, I invited him in for some cool lemonade. I couldn't help but notice his glistening, bronze, half naked body as he stretched the muscles on his arms and chest. He was well built, and once again I tingled all over. Somehow, wild images were racing through my mind, and I could almost feel him doing to me what I saw him doing to those other young girls. I ran my fingers along his bicep and scratched his arm with my fingernail. He bled a little, and I wiped the blood with my handkerchief." Rebecca continued to reminisce.

He was a little nervous and said, "Thank you, Missy Rebecca for the cool drink." As he started to walk away, he continued to say, "I must get back to work."

"At that moment, I ordered him to stop. I walked up to him and started to massage his muscular body and slowly moved my hands downward to unbuckle his pants."

He started to sweat and said, "Please, Missy Rebecca, I got to go. I can't stay here; it's too dangerous for me."

I ordered him to stay still as I explored the rest of his body. I closed my eyes and imagined that we were making mad passionate love. Suddenly he said, "Easy, you're hurting me," and I came back to reality.

I told him to follow me in to the side door that led into the den. I then closed the door and ordered him to take off his pants. He hesitated, and I hollered at him and said, "If you don't do what I tell you, I'll tell my Daddy that you raped me and you know what he will do to you. He will whip you hard, and then have you dumped in the cesspool pipe."

That's all I had to say because he took off his pants and stood there stark naked, just as I saw him by the pond that night. What a magnificent sight! I sat on the edge of the sofa and told him to come over to me.

He was very nervous, and I was getting more excited. I could feel his hand touch my inner thigh, and I experienced something so incredible my body went limp. Never in my whole life did I ever have this kind of feeling. My entire being felt like I had no control, and I trembled from my waist down to my toes. I continued to shake uncontrollably.

I instructed Henry to lie on my wanting naked body. He was a bit apprehensive but he did as he was told. I reached down and guided him, as I was anxiously waiting to be fulfilled. It wasn't long before his body participated fully, and for what seemed like an eternity, I was in a state of ecstasy like no other time in my entire life. It was the first good encounter that I have ever had, and I wasn't going to let this slip by me, now that I had him where I wanted him. I knew I could count on this experience whenever I wanted it, and there wasn't anything Henry could do about it except to participate. **Or else**, he knew very well what **or else** meant to him.

My Momma and Daddy would leave me alone in the house at least once a week while they did their errands or went visiting. They never questioned me as to why I did not want to go with them. They left me alone to myself. I would tell them that I had some reading to catch up on. I always looked forward to Momma's and Daddy's weekly trips because I knew I could order Henry up here. He would not hesitate to come because he knew if he didn't, he would be haunted by my threat to tell Daddy that he raped me. He was damned if he showed up and damned if he didn't show up. He had no choice in the matter, and that's how I kept control. I also warned him that if he didn't perform every time as good as the first time, he would be in serious trouble.

For over six months, Henry performed like an animal. There was no lovemaking; it was pure lust. I treated him just the way our stud horses were treated on the plantation....that was to perform without feelings. It was wonderful while the excitement lasted, but then I got bored.

It was only a matter of time, and I started spying again. Nobody ever caught me. There was this one beautiful light tan girl that Henry would meet almost every night. She would move her body, scream, twist, groan and moan, and dig her nails right into Henry's back. After a few times of watching this, I saw Henry do something different to her that he never did to me. One night I looked over the wall near the pond. I could see Millie, the light tan girl, lying naked on a blanket. Henry appeared a few minutes later. He stood at her feet and removed his clothing, and, as usual, I thought he would rest his body upon hers. Instead, he knelt down in front of her and began kissing every part of her body. I couldn't see what he was doing, but I could see what it was doing to Millie. Quietly moaning, she rolled from side to side and seemed to be enjoying this immensely. She grabbed his body and dug her fingernails deep into his skin and let out such a scream, it caused her to go limp. I got goose pimples all over my body as I witnessed this, and it became very difficult to keep my composure. The excitement was so overwhelming that I almost made my presence known. I couldn't wait until the next time Henry visited me, because he was going to perform this same act of lust for me.

The day finally arrived for Henry's visit, and, yet, he was unaware of what I had planned. He came in very slowly and timidly as he always did because he was still afraid of what I could do to him if he didn't cooperate. When he removed my undergarments and began to unbuckle his pants, I said, "Stop! Kneel down in front of me." He hesitated and I ordered him again. He knelt down slowly and began kissing me in places that I didn't know existed. Whatever he did made me go frantically wild.

He teased me beyond my wildest dreams and said, "I didn't bargain for this. I don't mind being your stud, but that's all I'll do."

I told him how I had spied on him and Millie and saw him doing the same thing to her. He was furious and said, "Anyone can do that to Millie!"

I ordered him to make mad passionate love to me, so I could reach the heights that Millie reached. Again, he drove me wild, but all I could think about over and over in my mind were the words he said, "Anyone can do that to Millie?" If that were so, maybe I could do that to Millie, too? It was a crazy thought, but if I could, how would I approach her or even get close to her? I want to drive her crazy like Henry did that night by the pool, and I must find a way to allow this to happen.

Millie was about five feet tall and weighed about 130 pounds, and she was only 16 years old. I was almost 18 years old, and I grew to 5' 10" and weighed 150 pounds. I was well built for my size and weight, especially for a woman. My problem was that I did not know how to get Millie to cooperate with me. After thinking about it, I asked Henry if he could set up a meeting between Millie and me. Henry agreed, but I had to release my hold on him. There would be no more sex and no more threats, and if I agreed to that, he would set up the meeting. I knew I had to make a decision quickly. It didn't take me long because I knew that if it did not work out, I could always get another stud. So Henry and I made a deal, and he agreed to set up the meeting.

I asked Henry's advice on how I could carry out my fantasy with Millie.

He replied, "Just go slow and easy; no roughing her up; kiss her as if you were making love and do what feels good to you. Do not hurt her."

Henry then set up the meeting for the following night. I couldn't wait for that night to arrive; it seemed to take forever. The air was warm and the time was 10:00 P.M. when I finally reached the designated area. Millie was lying naked on a blanket and Henry was lying beside her. He turned her head towards his lips and smothered her with kisses. At the same time, he slowly moved his hand down along her body and gently massaged her legs. His fingers moved up one side of her body and down the other side. He began kissing her neck, her shoulders, and moved slowly toward her wanting bosom. That was my cue to move in closer. Earlier, Henry told me not to touch her body with my hands, but to put my lips on her bare skin. I did exactly what he told me, and I moved my tongue lovingly all around her beautiful body. This was a first for me, and it was having quite an impact on my emotions.

Millie wasn't even aware of what was happening to her. The excitement of this encounter was beyond my wildest dreams, and I loved it. She had such a sweet aroma, and it turned me on even more. As I continued to kiss her over and over again, I had several orgasms, one after the other. This felt as good as, or even better than when Henry and I had sex.

At this point, Henry held her down by lying across her chest and continuously kissing her while I went even wilder with Millie. Millie was so hot and bothered, she didn't realize what was happening to her. Suddenly, she let out a screech and wriggled uncontrollably as she reached her ultimate climax. It had affected me so much, that I too exploded with wild feelings without even being touched. I believe that at 18 years old, I had experienced something that most women never experience in their lifetime....I had a sexual encounter with another woman.

Just as I got up to leave, Henry lied upon Millie's perspiring, hot body and continued on. When I got back to my bedroom, I bathed and went to bed. As I lay there, I realized that this night was going to have a great impact on me for the rest of my life. It was not natural for me to enjoy what I just took part in, and, yet, I couldn't get it out of my mind. I asked myself over and over again, how could this young girl of only 16 years of age make me feel this way?

I felt like an old woman who had just raped this little young girl. I appeared to be an amazon next to her small body. But it felt good, and I loved every moment of it.

A few weeks went by since that wild night with Millie, and because I made a deal with Henry, he kept his distance.

I wanted to get to know Millie better, so I decided to talk to her and ask if she would be willing to work as a housekeeper in the house, specifically to clean my room. In this manner, I could get close to her. It took me over a month before Millie began working in the house because I first had to convince my Daddy that I needed someone to take care of my room and to look after my belongings. He understood and was proud of the way I ordered the black servants around. If he only knew how I used them for my own personal advantage, he would drown me.

I was like a mink in heat; my body and mind had been tormented the last thirty days or so, and I wanted to be with Millie now.

«*XIII* »

Rebecca & Millie Meet Again

The week finally ended and I was again left alone in the big house. I asked Millie to bring in a pitcher of warm water so I could take a sponge bath. She carried the pitcher over to the basin and poured the warm water into it. I told her to come closer to me. By this time, I only had on my undergarments. I asked Millie to wet the sponge and pass it over my backside and shoulders and then down my neck to my lower back and across my buttocks. It felt so good; I knew what I was doing, but I did not want to scare Millie away from me. I asked her to wash my legs and then my chest. Millie slowly and gently passed the sponge over and around my firm breasts and then she passed over the sensitive areas. The more Millie bathed me, the more excited I became. She washed every part of my body, and at the same time, she was shaking all over. I then took the sponge out of her hand, set it in the basin, turned her around, unbuttoned her dress, and let it fall to the floor.

What a beautiful, shapely young body. I sat her down on the edge of the bed and removed her shoes and socks. I then took the sponge and washed her neck and shoulders. I unhooked her bra as I passed my hand over her sensuous back. Her breasts were round and firm and nice to the touch. I pushed her toward the bed. Her body was still shaking. I told her to relax because I was not going to hurt her. I ran the damp sponge across her plump bosom and became anxiously excited. This event, this young woman, made me feel as though I was the man of this house. I slowly pulled her panties down around her ankles and removed them. I then sponged her abdominal area and moved slowly downward toward her feet. I had hoped that she would become more relaxed; however, I sensed that she was slightly frightened to be with me. She was trembling, and I became even more excited. I put the sponge down and knelt at the edge of the bedside and began to kiss her feet, as I moved toward her thighs. I couldn't believe that this was happening all over again as I had hoped.

Our excitement was mutual and once again, I lost myself in the overwhelming ecstasy of the moment. Millie fainted and I regained my composure. Millie slowly regained consciousness, and I asked myself why was it that I loved having sex with Millie instead of having sex with Henry? I was confused and disturbed. When Millie finally came around, she realized what had just taken place and pulled me into her body with such force, and screamed, "Don't stop! Don't stop!"

In the excitement, for some reason, I grabbed my stockings and wrapped it around her neck and squeezed it real tight. Millie was now more frightened than she had ever been. I told her that if she ever told anyone that I had participated sexually with her, I would strangle her to death and throw her body into the cesspool pipe to rot with all the other Negroes. She promised me she would not say anything because she was going to run away. She said she felt disgraced and humiliated. She admitted that she, too, liked being fondled by another woman and that this was not morally right.

« XIV »

A Time to Reflect

Rebecca then said, "You see, Raffaele, I have never told anyone about this part of my life, and I don't know why I told it to you now."

I looked at Rebecca and said, "This is incredible. Do you expect me to believe what you just told me? You are a married woman with two children!"

Rebecca snapped back, "That doesn't mean anything. You heard me say that I liked being with a man as well, but not as much as what I had experienced with Millie. My husband and I don't have much sex. As a matter of fact, if I could get more weight off my body, I wouldn't mind asking you to have sex with me. You look like you could give me a good time and satisfy me the way Henry did."

Immediately, I responded to Rebecca and told her that I was a very happily married man with a wife and family and that I don't get involved with other women.

Rebecca then said, "Yeah, I could go for your wife, also. She's less than five feet and less than one hundred thirty pounds. I like them small. As a matter of fact, I like your wife's hair. I touched it a few times when I walked by her, and she didn't even know it. I even bought her a pretty blouse. I wanted her to wear it, but she couldn't accept it."

"Rebecca, did you indulge in anything before you came here tonight?"

"Like what? Coffee? Tea? Maybe you could like me."

"No, no. I mean did you smoke anything or take any narcotics?"

"I don't do drugs. That's bad for you. It can mess up your mind. I might not know what I'm doing, but I always know when I do something wrong."

I looked at my watch and was amazed at how the time had gone by. This woman had been talking to me for almost three hours. I asked her if she would like some coffee, and she said that she would enjoy a cup of coffee now. I went into the kitchen to put on a pot of coffee, and she hollered from the other room, "Do you think I am capable of murdering that woman, Doris? She keeps haunting my mind and repeats the words, "You murdered me! You murdered me!"

I walked back to where Rebecca was sitting and answered her, "I really don't know, Rebecca. It's kind of confusing. I am trying to get to know you, and I am attempting to understand you. You seem to go out of your way to help the underdog or the less fortunate. It's almost as if you were on a guilt trip, trying to make amends." It seems that at this time in Rebecca's life she spent a lot of time helping the less fortunate people in the community. I make this statement because I wonder what her reasons are if, in fact, she did have anything to do with Doris's murder. Could she be on a guilt trip?

Her response was, "Yes, I'd like to get to know you better, too. I'd love to have sex with you. Do you think if I fixed myself up, you could find me attractive enough to take me to a motel and have your way with me?"

"Rebecca, I told you I am not interested. I am heavily involved with a highly controversial subject relating to ghosts and spirits, and I don't need to get messed up by having an involvement with anyone."

Still trying, Rebecca said, "I'm going to help you make a lot of money, Raffaele. I can get my hands on a lot of video equipment so you can make movies and become rich and famous and have a lot of money."

"I don't need lots of money, Rebecca. I would like to get down to the truth concerning Doris and why you happen to be such an important part of the scenario."

The coffee was brewed, and I took it into the front room for Rebecca and me. We sat back drinking our coffee, and I asked her to continue with the story of her life as the years moved forward.

"Well", conceded Rebecca, "I enjoyed Henry and Millie alternately every other week for about two years."

"Wait, wait a minute. I thought you told me you released Henry from your clutches and Millie was going to run away."

"I know I told you that, but they both loved the arrangement with me as much as I did with them, so we continued for a while. Anyway, after that I decided to take a trip to Kentucky. I spent about three years just traveling. I could tell you wild stories about every place I went because

I feel that life is what you make of it. If you want to do something, no matter what, you should just do it. Don't worry your head over whether it is right or wrong or if someone will get hurt. I do what I want and when I want to do it."

"When did you first come to Massachusetts?"

"At first I went to Maine, somewhere near the Canadian border. It was right near a big river. I stayed there for a short while."

"But when did you come to Massachusetts, Rebecca?"

"I think it was back in 1965 or so. My cousin and I came together. She's a big girl also. She is a little bigger than me. We also look alike. I'll see if I can find a picture of us so you can see how much we look alike."

"Where is she now?"

"She's gone back down south where she likes it."

"How old were you when you came here?"

"Let's see....I was born in the year 1937. If I came here in 1965, I must have been about 28 years old. Yeah, I was a beautiful, sexy 28 year old woman. I never stopped enjoying sex. It didn't matter how I got it or who I was with as long as I got it. I'll always love it."

"Okay, so you're up here and you are 28 years old. What did you do up here? Where did you live? Did you work?"

"I did not work for a while. I have money; you know I came from a wealthy family," Rebecca boasted.

"Where did you live, Rebecca?"

"Around Brown Street, Myrtle Street, Ash Street, School Street, and Eddy Street,"

"You lived on all of those streets?"

"Since I've been here, I've moved around a lot. I don't stay in one house too long; I really miss the big house in Georgia."

"What do you do for excitement?"

"I'd go to some bars and have a drink or two. Maybe I'd get lucky and meet someone and have a one-night stand until the next time."

"Rebecca, before you answer this next question, I want you to think, think very hard. **Have you ever met a girl by the name of Doris in any of the bars that you visited? Take your time.**"

She took my advice and thought about the question that I had just posed to her. After a few seconds, she replied, "Yes! Yeah, I think that first year I came to Waltham there was a little girl I met in one of the bars on Main Street. Yes, a cute little one; I towered over her. She got a kick out of my southern accent and was sort of fascinated by it. Yeah, I remember we had a few drinks together. Come to think of it, she kind of reminded me of Millie, except she was white and well endowed. She always dressed very provocatively.

That's how I remember her. She loved drinking beer and had lots of male friends; almost my kind of lady."

"Did you ever see her after that first time in the bar?"

"No, but I think my cousin may have seen her. My cousin may have worked in the same plant with her."

"I thought you said your cousin went back down south?"

"Yeah, after about six to eight months."

"Rebecca, I thought you told me you could not drink because of a pancreas problem?"

"I can't now, but back then I could and I did."

"Did you ever take Doris out? Did you every go anyplace with her? Think hard and try to remember."

"No, I don't believe so. I would have remembered that because I would have had my way with her, and I would have enjoyed it immensely."

"You never, never saw her again after that time?"

"Well, maybe I did one more time at Ma's Place up on Main Street. I got to hold her when she stumbled into my arms after she tripped at the bar. She landed straight into my arms and on top of me. Her nose was between my breasts. But no, nothing ever happened between us; not that I would have rejected her. No way would I."

At this time, the hour was getting late, and I told Rebecca we could continue this talk some other night. She informed me that she felt a very strong impression that Doris was trying to take over her body and also her mind.

« *XV* »

Elimination of Suspects

The next day I gathered all my notes, and my associate Diane and I reviewed them in an attempt to sort out a few facts. We believed this woman was very strong and capable of killing someone. After all, she did meet the deceased during her first year that she lived here. She was attracted to Doris because she reminded her of the servant girl, Millie, and we know exactly what kind of a relationship she had with her. The odd thing is that Millie was 16 years old and Rebecca was a few years older. Doris was 46 years old and Rebecca was 28 years old, which made her younger than Doris. This was a switch. One girl was younger and the other much older. By Rebecca's own admission, she was bisexual. So what would the connection or motive be if she indeed were the one who strangled Doris on the morning of August 16, 1967?

Shorty did not recognize her picture and neither did Rebecca recognize Shorty's picture, but in the trance state when Doris occupies the body and mind of Rebecca, she then recognizes Shorty just as if they were out together again. Rebecca told us she did not drink now, and, yet, she also told us during one of our sessions that in her younger days, she drank.

We needed to get more information about Doris's life and her involvement with those men who have been accused of strangling her. It seemed very easy to fit a motive to every one of them. Her first husband is deceased so we can eliminate him as a subject. She was divorced from her second husband for over ten years, and at the time of her death, he had a girlfriend. They lived out of state and only saw Doris when they came in town to visit friends and most of the times they were in the bars. Therefore, what could be his motive to strangle Doris? He could also be ruled out. However, he gave a statement to the police that could make you think otherwise. He said he drove by Doris's house at 5:30 p.m. on August 15, and that was the night before she was strangled. Why and for what reason did they drive by the house? It was out of the way to any of the bars they might visit. Based on this statement, maybe he should not be ruled out yet. The owner of the café, Frank, was always tending the bar whenever Doris came in, and he always stayed there until closing time. Frank always noticed when she left the bar. He was never sure if Doris was going home or elsewhere. Leroy Manning was also a customer of the café. He and Doris would always talk over a drink even though he was known to be a very shy person, and, yet, he was very friendly to Doris. He had a stuttering problem that kept him from conversing as easily as most people do. He lived within walking distance from the bar and would walk to the café and later would walk home. Since he did not own an automobile, he was never known to date Doris. It seems as though their friendship remained within the café. According to police records, Doris's daughter believed that Walter Norton was Doris's date the night of August 15, 1967. However, she claimed he never showed up, and Doris went to the café alone. Her house was less than one half mile to the main road where every bar, grille, and café was located.

Walter lived in the next town and would occasionally drive over to have a few drinks with Doris about twice a week. When they finished drinking for the evening, they would sometimes go parking. He would not take her anywhere special, but would drive around town, maybe have a little more to drink and then head right over to the duck pond where they would park and, if he was lucky, become romantically involved. I say lucky because if Doris had too much to drink, she could be too drunk to participate in any sexual activity.

Norton, Manning, and Johnson had all taken lie detector tests and passed favorably. William T. Dunn had dated Doris for five years even though he knew Doris was having sex with other men. This bothered him, but would it have bothered him enough to kill her?

Dick Freni was an entrepreneur and was successful to some extent. He loved drinking, and he loved his women. He had known Doris for over 5 years also and dated her from time to time. He had money, boats, marinas, women, and, yes, he even had a wife. He enjoyed doing everything in a big way and was very determined in everything that he did. Doris had also worked for him part time doing bookkeeping. He could have sex with her anytime he wanted. He could have been jealous of the other men in her life or maybe Doris was stealing from him. Let's not rule out the possibility that Doris could have threatened to tell his wife, Madeline Freni, about her relationship with her husband and their escapades. However, that would be a form of blackmail. There was a lot of information that could make him the number one suspect.

After this, it was not clear if Doris left Freni or if Freni left Doris when Steve Bergin came into the picture. Steve was believed by many to be one of the last men in Doris's life. Could Steve have been jealous over the fact that Doris had many sexual lovers? Assuming that he knew of them, would it be enough to push him over the edge to kill her? Doris provoked Steve and flaunted all her lovers in front of him and teased him in such a way that he could not match up to any of them. For some men this could bust their ego enough for them to want to kill. So it would seem as the facts are being revealed that the prime suspects would be

Freni as number one, Norton as number two, and Bergin as number three.

It is also puzzling because according to some, Doris was a very friendly woman and had many friends, so why would anyone want to hurt her? Most of the so-called friends were men who made good use of her by abusing her and taking sexual advantage of her. It seems that she was also somewhat of a responsible person for she was raising two children and holding down a full-time job. Everyone at the factory agreed that she was a steady, hard worker. She never complained and always did what she was instructed to do. She was never late, and regardless of the fact that she drank excessively, she was always sober on the job, always on time, and put in a full hard day's work. She was well liked by everyone at the factory.

It is safe to say that she did not have any enemies in her life, and, yet, someone did strangle her to death. It had to have been someone she knew and trusted in order for that person to get close enough to her to be able to wrap a silk stocking around her neck and, yes, even to be able to remove the silk stockings from the body to do this. Over the next several months, an attempt was made to interview anyone and everyone who worked at the factory or knew the woman known as Doris.

« *XVI* »

Rebecca Reaches Out

Also, some research was conducted to further understand the woman known as Rebecca. She was a startling and unique woman who also had the capability of being very dangerous. Rebecca revealed that she had worked in an institution for the violent and mentally disturbed. While on the job, she had been beaten up a few times. Unexpectedly, one patient bit her under her armpit that ultimately became infected. At a later time, during another confrontation with a patient, someone viciously bit off her thumb.

With all of my conversations with Rebecca, she seemed to enjoy the company of young people at least twenty to thirty years her junior. I don't know if guilt played a big part in Rebecca's life because she would always go out of the way to help the less fortunate, including young people who found themselves in trouble. Her intentions were meant well, but her involvement became such that she would participate with drugs and illicit sex. She also made claim that she would watch and observe others as they indulged in lustful acts of lovemaking while sober, drunk, or on drugs. From time to time, she would bring young, sixteen to eighteen year old girls with her to my office claiming they had been possessed by evil, the Devil, and claiming it was in their bellies. She also had them convinced the only way to get rid of this evil was to have sex. All the girls she brought over seemed to be of Spanish origin and spoke very little English.

She said that the Spanish people believed wholeheartedly in spirits, be they evil or good. Rebecca seemed to win them over, and they believed her and wanted the evil out of their bellies. I told them that they should go to their church and speak to the priest for I could not help them.

Another time she brought a young girl about fourteen years old to my office saying that she was having trouble in school, and her reading skills were far below the level of her age group due to a dyslexia problem. Rebecca had her convinced that I could conjure up the spirits to deliver to her a magic key, and it would help to improve her reading skills. Rebecca meant no harm; she was trying to help the young girl who was having a rough time in school. Rebecca succeeded in making me feel sorry for the young lady, so I decided to talk to her. She seemed to be very easily influenced by suggestions, so I attempted to use hypnosis on a level with much less intensification. I proceeded to tell her that the spirits she was feeling were placed in her head for the purpose of helping her with reading and schoolwork, and whenever she needed help, all she had to do was to close her eyes for a few seconds and visualize this bright red magic key. I told her all she had to do was to see herself turning on the key mentally and the spirits would help her instantly. She understood all that I had implanted as suggestion with such enthusiasm. She thanked me and agreed to follow my instructions.

A few weeks later, I received a call from the girl's teacher. She wanted to know what I did to this girl to have caused such a miraculous turnaround and rapid improvement in her reading skills. She wanted to know just what this magic was all about. I told the teacher it worked because the girl had a friend by the name of Rebecca who took an interest in wanting to help her, and I only used hypnosis together with keyed suggestions. The teacher found this to be amazing and said she wanted to learn more about this later on. I only mention this incident because it showed that Rebecca had a good side, and I don't know if it was spurned on by guilt or if it was an honest and sincere effort on her part.

The young girl went on to graduate and became quite the young lady, and I believed that Rebecca's effort played an important role in her life because of her desire to help others. Does this sound like the profile of someone who would viciously strangle another human being?

Another incident occurred a short while later, and I believe it will also show that there are two directions to consider before arriving at a decision as to what is the force that is guiding Rebecca. Is it her deep guilt? Is it actually the spirit of Doris?

« *XVII* »

The Torment Continues

I had received a phone call from Rebecca. She wanted to know if she could come by the office to have a chat with me. I told her to come over even though I thought this was a little strange. In the past, if she wanted to talk to me, she would just come over and bang on my door no matter what time of day or night; mostly between 9:00 p.m. and 2:00 a.m. When she arrived, I noticed a very neatly dressed woman, and she was behaving somewhat indifferent. She said that she was disturbed and was experiencing a nervous jittery feeling. I asked her how her day went and if there was anything unusual that had taken place this day or any other day since the last time we met which was about one week ago. She said she felt jumpy. Something was wrong, but she could not pin it down. She very bluntly asked how I felt about her and if I found her attractive enough to want to go out with her.

I explained, as I had in the past, that I did not have an interest in going out with anyone. However, I thought she was a nice woman, and I was pleased to see that she was helping people, especially that young girl with the dyslexia problem.

She wanted to know if I would allow Doris to use her body so she could talk to me. She said she felt that Doris wanted to speak to me since last week. I asked if she had allowed Doris to come in recently, and she said that she was fighting to keep her out. It was against my better judgment, but I was tempted to let Doris come in because I was curious as to why Rebecca wanted her to talk to me. Normally, I would not work with anyone unless I had a witness present to observe what takes place. Being close to midnight, I could not call anyone, so I put on my reliable tape recorder and lowered the telephone answering machine so we would not be abruptly disturbed.

Rebecca asked for a glass of water, sat down, and said she was ready. It did not take long to establish a rapport, and in less than a few minutes, Doris was doing the talking.

Her opening words were, "Well, I guess I taught this bitch a lesson this week!"

I asked Doris if she could explain what she meant since her statement was so strong and positive.

With a vengeance in her voice, Doris said, "I'll screw her up one side and down the other before I'm through with her for what she did to me!" She then started singing these words, "Roll, roll, roll your head gently down the street, merrily, merrily, merrily see if you can get away with this feat." She stopped and repeated these words very slowly,

"Today we got one; maybe tomorrow we'll get two. Let me help her. It's what you want me to do."

This was not making any sense to me. I told her to stop being silly and start making some sense when she talked.

She said, "Oh, I'm making very good sense, but you don't know our Rebecca like I do, do, do. I am going to drive this woman crazy and finally kill her for what she did to me!"

Doris began talking about a friend of Rebecca's who had just beheaded somebody. Doris claimed she was in the car when it was done, and she would aid Rebecca in helping the young kids who hit the man and caused his head to just keep rolling down the road. I told her that I did not understand much of what she was saying. Doris called me a stupid idiot and accused me of not paying attention to her words.

She said, "What am I to do? Draw a map for you? I'm going to let you in on a secret. There was another murder committed this week, and you can't figure it out. There was a hit and run accident where the driver of the vehicle hit a man on the highway. The impact was so great that the victim's head came right of his shoulders and it rolled down the road."

I couldn't believe my ears. Is this what Doris meant when she said, "Roll, roll, roll your head gently down the street?" She also told me the occupants of the car fled from the scene of the accident, and they looked to Rebecca for help. This delighted Doris because she was controlling Rebecca to the point where it would eventually mess up her life. At that moment, Rebecca woke up abruptly — startled and disturbed. She asked what happened, what Doris said, and what Doris wanted from her.

"Why can't I hear her, Raffaele?" asked Rebecca. I told Rebecca to relax and remain calm.

I repeated, "Nothing has happened. Doris still wants to get even with you for something you did to her. Can you think of anything you may have done to her that could upset her as much?"

She boisterously said, "Hey, I've lived a full life. I may have hurt many unintentionally without realizing it, but I'm trying to make up for a lot of that by helping others."

These words reflected a person who was wrestling with her conscious mind over good and evil. It seemed as though she was trying to make amends for her past. However, her past still remained a mystery to us. What could she have done to make Doris so upset and so mad at her?

Were her actions that of a voluntary or involuntary nature? Did she hurt by inflicting wounds on others or was it more emotional rather than physical? This case was evolving into a very intriguing one, and it became necessary for us to find the answers.

Without warning, Rebecca got up and said, "Good night, Raffaele. I'll talk with you later on." She did not tell me for sure if she was involved in the accident.

« XVIII »

Trouble for Rebecca

A few days later, I heard from Rebecca by phone. She asked if I could use hypnosis to help someone forget a terrible act that took place in his life. Somehow, I just knew this had to be related to the hit and run accident in which Doris claimed Rebecca was involved. I answered her by saying that it would depend on the strength of the act, how deep it was imbedded into the mind, and how long it had been there. I also asked if it was a deep guilt or just something this person wanted to forget. She said it was or could be something terrible and that it could have an affect on this person for the rest of his life.

I commented to Rebecca. "If it is that terrible, it could only be an act of rape or murder." Rebecca was very quiet for a moment. Suddenly, she blurted out, "I've got to go. I'll talk to you later," and then she hung up the phone.

It then became easier to put some of the pieces together. What Rebecca said the other night and what she just said on the phone now gave me some of the clues I needed. Did Rebecca know the occupants of the vehicle involved in the hit and run? Did they confide in her or was she with them in the vehicle at the time of the incident? Remember what Doris said? She claimed she was in the car when it happened. Was she there in the spirit sense or was she there within the body and mind of Rebecca? There were many times Rebecca did not realize that Doris had taken possession of her body until she got home from a wild spree.

To what extent would Rebecca go to help them cover up the crime, assuming they were involved in the hit and run accident? To what extent would Doris force Rebecca to do right or wrong? As far as I could see, all of the information was from a mysterious side of Rebecca while she was being controlled without her knowledge, and the rest came from a frantic woman on the telephone. I pretty much came to the conclusion that I had to classify this information as hearsay until I could confirm all of this. I decided to sit on this and wait it out until I could see what their (Doris and Rebecca's) next move would be.

Meanwhile, I decided to call a friend of mine who was on the Waltham police force and asked him if he could find out if there had been a hit and run reported. He called me back the next day and said there were no hit and runs reported locally, however, the Metropolitan police had a report on file about a veteran who had been hit on a major highway and was decapitated. Bingo…a hit!!! He also told me there were no available clues as to what had happened, but he still wanted to know what I knew about it. This incident was out of my friend's jurisdiction. I told him I would get back to him later because I had to do more research and get more answers. He knew I did a lot of research in the spiritual area of the paranormal. He again asked if the information was from the spirit world or was it information I had from reliable physical sources. I joked with him and told him my information came from the ghosts with whom I communicate. He reminded me that this is serious business because the hit and run now involved a dead man's body. It could be classified as murder and anyone withholding information could be considered an accessory to the fact.

Joking again, I said, "How could you ever go to your superiors and tell them a ghost told you about the hit and run incident? They would think you needed a long vacation."

I knew my friend was speaking to me in this manner for my benefit to make me aware of the law. Again, I thanked him and told him I would get back to him when I had something more concrete that he could research out. I hung up the phone and sat back in my chair, closed my eyes, and thought, "What do I really have here?" Rebecca is a frantic woman who feels that she is being haunted by the spirit of a promiscuous female who was strangled to death and she accuses Rebecca of killing her.

It is also obvious that some young friends of Rebecca's could be in trouble or she could be in trouble with them. It seems that there was a report about a man who was the victim of a hit and run accident in which he lost his head. Because I heard about that report, these words flashed before my eyes, "Roll, roll, roll your head gently down the street." I can remember those words surprisingly coming from Doris. It would now seem to me that Rebecca might know a lot more about this than what she was actually

revealing to me.

« *XIX* »

The Cover Up

Another week went by, and one morning, about 2:00 a.m., I heard a loud banging on the front door of my office. I opened the door and it was Rebecca. She was frantically banging the door with her clenched fist. She looked as though she had seen a ghost. I got her a glass of water and calmed her down long enough to speak. Then she started to tell me what made her panic so. It seems that she had found herself at the brook where Doris was strangled. She said that she felt compelled, as if she was being forced. Her sneakers were wet, and there was mud on her socks and slacks as well. I drew the conclusion that she had gone into the water. But why would she do that? I asked her why she went down to the brook alone at night.

Rebecca was distraught, upset, and confused. She hysterically cried, "I do not know why I went. I just did."

I assured her that she would be all right and suggested to her that it would be best if she went home and got a good night's sleep and early tomorrow night, not at 2:00 a.m., we would discuss this again. Furthermore, I was too tired to do anything, especially since I did not have any witnesses, and I knew that I couldn't call anyone at this hour. I could just picture it now if I were to call someone at 2:00 a.m. and said, "Why don't you get out of bed and come to my office to witness a session with this frantic woman, Rebecca." They would not take kindly to it, let alone think I was crazy and as psychotic as the woman.

Early the following night, Rebecca came over and wanted to talk about her friend's problem, not realizing that she could be part of the problem. She did not know how or where to start or begin. I told her to start from the beginning when she first received the call from her friend. Did her friend call to go for a joy ride or was he seeking advice? I reminded her that it would be very helpful if she could remember if that was the first time they talked about the incident or was there a time before? I knew I could use hypnosis and put her back in time to get at the truth, but I couldn't be sure if Doris would just jump in at any time and try to confuse the story. So, I hesitated to think about using hypnosis. It could make it difficult to distinguish true statements from false, and it would also be difficult to determine who was partaking of the conversation, which is why I felt it best if Rebecca could relate on her own volition.

She seemed to be jumping around with her story. She was rambling on and on about two young Spanish kids in a car. She also mentioned something about beer being in the car, as well as paraphernalia and articles that belonged to them. Then she talked about how to hide the evidence, how to make it look like someone stole the car and then telling them to go home and instructing them that she had to go with them so they wouldn't botch up the plan.

Finally, I interjected and said, "Slow down. You're not making any sense. Start again. You mentioned two young kids. Can you identify them and reveal what they said to you?"

She became nervous and asked, "Are you going to the police with what I am going to tell you?"

I assured her that, so far, I didn't see any crime or evidence of criminal activity relative to her as of now. I also assured her that if it became necessary to notify the authorities, I would discuss it with her first. and if I believed what she was going to reveal to me, then I would discuss it with her before I notified any authorities.

She went on speaking, "I am mixed up in the head, and I don't know what's real or what's not real anymore. I feel as though I am being haunted by the dead girl's spirit, and it is ruining my behavior. I just don't know what's happening to me. I don't know if I'm talking to you with my own mind or if it is her spirit who is talking to you."

A few hours went by and she still was having a hard time trying to remember in detail all of what she wanted to tell me. She finally agreed to allow me to hypnotize her and regress her back to when she was with the two young kids. Rebecca was very cooperative and very relaxed and allowed herself to respond with a receptive attitude. It only took two minutes for her to enter into a very deep sleep. At the same time, I was watching for any tell-tale signs of Doris so there would not be any interference from her.

When I felt she was ready, I suggested to her, "Think back to when you were with the two young kids. Are you with them or are they seeking you out for your help and advice?"

It seemed as though she was struggling to speak. She then began to speak very slowly, "There was a telephone call, and they wanted me to meet with them in the parking lot on Crescent Street. I asked them what they wanted to talk about. They sounded nervous and frightened. They wanted to know when we were going to put the plan into action. I told them not to move from their house, and I would be there in twenty minutes. When I arrived, they both were crying and appeared to be very hyper and excited."

They both spoke at once and said, "Are you sure you can help us? We don't know if we killed someone tonight. Do you know? We should not have been drinking. We really weren't speeding. All of a sudden, there was a big thump. You must have heard it, too. That happened when we drove under the bridge. We don't know if someone jumped off the bridge or was pushed off. We only saw a body drop right in front of the car. It came out of nowhere, and I think we hit it. It wasn't our fault. It just happened in a flash and, bingo, the body bounced off the car."

Rebecca said she tried to calm the boys down. She told the boys to drive the car and follow her to a spot in the parking lot where she could examine the car closely for any damages. Upon her examination, she discovered there was a piece missing from a small section of the front headlight. Everything else seemed to be intact. She told them to leave the car there and get into her car. Her brain was working overtime, for she was trying to find a way out for the kids and keep herself out of it as well.

After driving around town for a few hours, she had what she considered a brainstorm, and she explained it to the two boys. They agreed with her and proceeded to put the plan into motion. It was quite simple, so they thought. She explained, "We have to make it look like your car was stolen from the slum area of Waltham."

They drove to the most troubled and roughest area of the city. They grabbed articles that belonged to the Spanish inhabitants of the area, such as someone's hat, jacket, sweater, a newspaper, empty beer bottles and cans. They went back to the car in the parking lot and scattered these items around the back seat of the car with a few condoms, undergarments, and threw a pair of high-heeled shoes on the floor. She said a friend lent her a dent puller so they could yank out the keyhole and door locks to make it appear as though the car had been broken into. The plan was to make it look like a group of young teenagers stole the car, drank beer, had plenty of sex while driving around the city, hoping the end result would be that when the car was found, these same teenagers would be accused of the hit and run. The plan seemed flawless, and it was executed just as

Rebecca laid it out. To add more authenticity to the plan, they ditched the car in a parking area in Boston, went back to the same slum area of town, and co-mingled with some of the gangs that they knew. They participated with them in smoking pot, sniffing cocaine, and drinking beer. Their intent was to make it look as if they were there all night, and, when they were ready to leave, they would claim they could not find their car because someone stole it.

They called the police to report the stolen car so the time and date would be logged into their records. They lied to the authorities, giving them the wrong time. They gave the time as one hour before the hit and run took place, so if the time was tied to the hit and run, it would seem that the teenagers who stole the car also hit the man. Everything seemed to be going along perfectly.

When Rebecca woke up from the session, she had no idea of what she had revealed to me. She again asked if I could help her friends with this problem. I told Rebecca I had to think about this because it was no simple task; it involved a hit and run where somebody got murdered. Rebecca got upset and wanted to know how I found this out.

"Was it Doris who told you?" she threw back at me.

I said, "I don't know if it was the spirit of Doris who exposed your participation or your own guilt feeling of being involved."

She begged me not to go to the police with this story. I told her to go home, and I would do the same. I instructed her not to talk to anyone else about this. Not realizing that while in trance, she revealed information related to the hit and run and asked if she could tell me how she was connected to the accident. She alleged that she was only a passenger in the car. She related that the boys told her if she could help them out of this incident, they would be in agreement that she was never there and did not have any involvement whatsoever. I told her not to say any more and explained to her that whatever she reported to me would be treated confidentially. However, if it involved an illegal act or a crime of violence, I would have to seek out advice from the authorities as to what action should be taken. Rebecca begged me not to go to the police. Then suddenly she dropped a bombshell. Rebecca informed me that she was dying of cancer and only had a few years to live and did not want to live her remaining years in jail.

Rebecca looked up at me and affirmed, "I really wasn't there, Raffaele. I was not involved. I only wanted to help the kids."

Immediately, as if possessed, a second voice cried out, "You were so there because I was there, and if I was there, I'm with you so you were there." This outburst solidified that Doris and Rebecca, spiritual and physical, share the same corporeal body.

Upset by what she just heard, Rebecca stormed out of my office without a word spoken. It had been a long night, and I was tired and decided to go home. I thought that if Rebecca was in the car at the time of the hit and run accident, could it have been possible that Rebecca did murder Doris seventeen years ago as Doris claimed.

That night lying in bed, as I tried to go to sleep, I was restless and disturbed because I kept thinking about how I was going to reveal to my friend at the police station what I was told. It was at a point now that I had to confide in someone who was familiar with the law, but how? The story sounds so bizarre. Could it be true? Was Rebecca involved with this hit and run that she claimed was an accident? It would also seem that the accident was not premeditated, and their only fault would be that they left the scene. Was Rebecca telling the truth when she said she was not involved? She also said she was there as a passenger. However, Doris was adamant and claimed that she and Rebecca were both there. Exhausted, I finally drifted off to sleep.

« XX »

Raffaele Meets with the Police

The following day the local papers carried a story about a hit and run accident in which a decapitated man was found in the middle of the street under or near the bridge. No clues were available, and the body was not yet identified. It was later learned that the dead man was a Vietnam veteran. A few weeks went by and still the police reported no clues yet found.

I called my friend at the police station and asked him to call me from a private phone line. He did call and I told him I thought we should meet for coffee that night and I would fill him in on what information I had obtained since the last time we spoke. He also told me he had some information about the hit and run. The body was identified, and he would tell me about it at the coffee shop. I asked him not to tell anyone else that we were meeting because I wanted to keep it confidential.

At 8:00 p.m. we met at Dunkin' Donuts. He told me that the M.D.C. (Metropolitan Police) had an identification of the body killed in the hit and run. He was a 42 year old unemployed, decorated Vietnam veteran named Jack R. Humphreys. It was figured that the incident took place on Sunday, November 11, 1984, on or about 2:30 a.m. beneath the Western Avenue bridge on Soldiers Field Road in Brighton. This seemed to fit in with my information. I did not reveal any names to my friend at this time and told him I would meet with my messenger within a couple of days and attempt to force out of her the names, places, and possible time.

He then asked what the status was regarding the Doris Johnson case. I replied that we were at a standstill because of this hit and run tragedy. He wanted to know if I came to a conclusion about the Johnson case. I commented that at this time it appeared I had a frantic woman on my hands who believes to be haunted by the spirit of a deceased young woman by the name of Doris Johnson. This alleged spirit insists that her life was ended abruptly by strangulation with her own silk stocking. She accuses this woman whose body she has possessed to be the murderer. Based on the facts to date, I was beginning to believe that Rebecca did murder Doris. My friend felt that as a police officer, he would have to report this to the Chief of Police. However, he needed more concrete evidence. I assured him that at our next session, I would attempt to learn as much as I could about the hit and run case, as this would give us some insight as to the mindset of the alleged murderer, Rebecca. If in the session it can be proven that Rebecca indeed was involved in the hit and run, and then it could be true that the story is coming from her subconscious mind and not of a spirit, which would indicate that she probably murdered Doris Johnson. On the other hand, if it's not her subconscious mind but a true spirit entity entering Rebecca's body and mind, then it is very possible that the spirit of Doris influenced Rebecca to be in the car with the kids at the time of the hit and run. It also appears that Doris's spirit is attempting to drive Rebecca crazy to the point where she would confess to strangling Doris to death on August 16, 1967. Regardless of the facts, Rebecca cannot bring herself to accept that she did wrong in both cases. It was important to establish a profile of Rebecca in order to determine the state of her mind in both instances.

When my friend left that night, he was intrigued with our conversation, but, at the same time, he found it to be all too confusing. He would anxiously wait to hear from me, and hoped I would have more concrete information to clear

up any confusion he might have.

« XXI »

Doris Lets the Cat Out of the Bag

It was less than a week later when I received a phone call from Rebecca. She wanted to know if we were going to meet after weight class again this week to continue our experimenting in the psychic world. I told her that I would be looking forward to our next meeting. She asked me if I thought she was crazy or confused. I assured her that I did not think she was crazy, but I found her interesting.

She responded as always, "Interesting enough to go out with me?"

I answered emphatically, "No! Rebecca, I told you a dozen times, no!"

She came back with, "What about your wife? Can I go out with her?" I objected and said, "The answer is the same,

Rebecca. No!" My wife is four feet eleven inches tall and weights about 117 pounds, which is typical of the type of woman to which Rebecca was attracted.

Here you can recognize that Rebecca is still obsessed with little girls and women much younger than herself, which is part of her modus operandi even to this day. Out of the clear blue, she then asked if Steven, one of the younger males in our class, was available. Steven was a well-constructed male. Not only was he very handsome, but he had a magnetic personality. My advice to Rebecca was that she would have to ask Steven herself. My conversation with Rebecca was abruptly ended because, as usual, she was in a hurry.

As time progressed and the more psychic classes we had, I realized that many of my former clients were returning because they heard how interesting these classes and this particular case had become. My observation proved to be true later. The weight class ended about 9:00 P.M., and we were preparing to set up the room for the psychic class. About ten of my clients stayed as usual, but it became evident that at least a dozen more people had arrived to observe and participate. We locked the front door and told all those who were there (about twenty-five) to cooperate by being quiet and not to interfere or ask any questions unless I opened up the session to the class.

Rebecca sat down and did not seem nervous despite the large viewing audience. She turned to me and said, "I'm ready when you are, Raffaele."

I proceeded as usual with the same preparation of incantation. I asked for safety and protection from God in what we seek and all that is presented be truthful so that we may be instrumental in reaching a resolution to a justified end. It seemed to take a little longer on this night in getting Rebecca to enter into a deep rapport.

Without warning and from a quiet stillness, a voice rang out loud and clear, "I am here." Rebecca's body was twitching and rocking back and forth, as if the spirit of Doris was restless or maybe it was Rebecca's conscious mind giving Doris's spirit a difficult entry.

After some general conversation, I asked Doris how she felt, and if she had anything to discuss with us this evening. She seemed to become more relaxed and accepted Rebecca's body as the host. I then opened up by asking about the car accident. Doris responded by telling us that Rebecca would have us believe that she was not in the car when the body got hit.

She continued and said, "Remember, if I was there, she had to be there because I go nowhere without her, and it will be that way until I get my revenge for what she did to me."

Doris then made a very strong point claiming that Rebecca would try to convince us that she is confused about the hit and run. She urged us not to believe Rebecca. I asked Doris directly, "Were you with her that night in the car when the accidental hit and run took place?"

Doris answered, "I not only was there with her, but I haunted her into doing things that will eventually destroy her by feeding into her mind strong feelings of suggestions of any and or negative actions that could hurt her and attempt to trip her up. I did this even if it meant involving those persons who were with her or in her presence no matter where she was."

Diane stopped her note taking and abruptly asked, "Doris, if you were in the car with Rebecca, you should be able to tell me who else was in the car."

"Well," she responded, "there were two young teenagers. I heard the oldest one referred to as Mike. As usual, Rebecca seems to patronize young people. These two teenagers were at least 25 years younger than her."

I asked Doris if she could give an account of what happened. She continued, "We were picked up by the kids on Crescent Street, and they took us for a joy ride. The kids were drinking to the point where they seemed to be drunk, laughing and joking. Rebecca offered them a joint as they entered on the Massachusetts Turnpike heading toward Boston. They talked about going to the Common."

Doris went quiet for a few minutes, and the room was so still you could hear a pin drop. All of a sudden, Doris hollered, "Bang! There was a big bang and a thump. The car hit something or someone." Mike yelled, "Oh, shit! Something fell on the car. I think we ran over it."

Doris continued to describe what happened. She said Mike turned off at the next exit and headed back to the parking lot from where they began their joy ride. Rebecca told the boys to go home and we went home also. A few hours later, Rebecca got together with the boys in the Crescent Street parking lot, examined the car, and then laid out her plan before them. They accepted her plan and executed it exactly the way she explained it. Doris said she was with her when they drove the car to the underground parking garage. Rebecca followed them to Boston after they gathered all the evidence they needed to plant in the rear of the car. After they parked the car as planned, salted the evidence, and tore out the ignition switch and door locks, they got into Rebecca's car and drove back to Waltham. They went to the Felton Street area and partied all night – drinking, smoking pot, and indulging in sex. When they were ready to leave, they went out to the car, but immediately went back in and told everyone that the car had been stolen. They called the police and got the report on record at least one hour before the accident had taken place.

This way it would be easy for the police to put the blame elsewhere and hold someone else responsible for the hit and run. The boys never mentioned Rebecca's name and kept her out of it as though she was never at the scene of the crime.

I asked Doris what the make and color of the car was that they drove. Doris said, "It was a fairly new car, and it was blue."

Rebecca's body was moving around in the chair as if she were uncomfortable, as if she were struggling within herself. All of a sudden, her eyes popped wide open, and she looked around.

Startled, Rebecca asked, "Why is everyone looking at me? Is something wrong?"

She was now completely awake and had no recollection as to what had been revealed to us. The evening session ended, but everyone in the audience had at least a hundred questions. What we just heard seemed too incredible to be true. Was it real or fabricated? Did it come by a true spirit identity or was it from the guilt-ridden subconscious of a frantic woman?

« *XXII* »

Guess Who's Coming to Dinner

The next morning I called my friend from the Police Department and told him we should meet to go over some incredible information. We met for lunch, and I went over last night's session with him. I outlined what I thought had been presented. My friend listened intently as I went on. Apparently, Rebecca was in the car with the two young teenagers. They continued to drink to the point of intoxication, a marijuana joint was introduced to them, and they headed into Boston via the Massachusetts Turnpike. As they were driving, something or someone was in front of them. They hit it and headed back home to Waltham where a plan was put into action. Rebecca devised the plan, providing that the two boys would not involve her and divulge that she was present. They then drove the car to a parking garage in Boston. After a short time, they drove to Felton Street in Waltham and co-mingled with some Spanish people. They left to go home, but immediately returned inside and announced that their car had been stolen. They called the police to report a stolen car so it would be on record, but lied about the time being one hour earlier so that it would be believed that the people who stole the car did the hit and run accident.

My friend looked at me and said, "Boy, if this is right, this is incredible! Were you given any names, places, kind of car, etc.?"

I told my friend that the oldest one of the two was called Mike, and the car was a blue, late model car. He wanted to see the stolen car report first before he rode into Boston to look for a blue car with broken door locks.

He did his homework and was in contact with the M.D.C. Police. He used the clues I gave him from our so-called spirit and guilt-ridden individual. His investigation turned out to be successful, and he was commended for work beyond the call of duty. On December 1, 1984, an article read in a local newspaper, *Waltham man charged in hit-and-run death. Michael Devlin has been summoned to answer the complaints. Jack R. Humphreys, 42, from Concord, was struck by a car on November 11, 1984 and was pronounced dead at St. Elizabeth's Hospital.*

Rebecca seemed to escape any involvement with the hit and run accident. I was left with two scenarios: (1) Did all that was exposed come from the sub-conscious mind of Rebecca because of deep guilt, or (2) Assuming Doris did cause all the problems, did she also allow Rebecca to be freed from any punishment of involvement? If you believe #2, then how does Doris get her revenge? If you believe #1, then there is no spirit of Doris, just Rebecca's guilt, and she, indeed, could have killed Doris.

I believed the time had come for the truth to be told. I would either have to force the guilt from Rebecca or the spirit of Doris would have to come forward. I let a couple of weeks go by before we had another session. Rebecca called me almost every other day or night, telling me that Doris will not leave her alone; that she was being driven crazy, and she wasn't feeling very well. She said that Doris was forcing her to do a lot of crazy things that she wouldn't normally do. She was forcing her to use her plastic credit card at the ATM machine to get free money to buy clothes and eat out. Doris seemed to be getting a stronger hold on Rebecca. If it was revenge she wanted, what could she be thinking? She could have created a situation whereby it could have forced the kids to implicate Rebecca in the hit and run. However, she didn't because it appeared that Doris wanted Rebecca dead.

One night about 11:00 p.m., I got a call from Rebecca. She told me that she was at the Chinese restaurant on Main Street and wanted to know if I could meet her there. I said I would be there shortly. When I got there, Rebecca seemed to be a little high. I didn't know if it was from drinking booze or smoking pot. She was at a table for four, and she sat against the wall on the left side across from two other women. They both had mixed drinks and also talked as if they were drunk as well. I sat next to Rebecca, and when the waiter came, she attempted to order the food. She slurred her words in a mixed up fashion which made it difficult for the waiter to understand her.

She would say, "I'll have pork strips," and as soon as she said that, the next line was, "No, you won't have that. You will have ribs." It was as if there was an echo in the room. If it was Doris, it was sort of disguised or muffled because Rebecca was high. I witnessed what appeared to be two individuals sharing the same body and arguing with one another as to what food would be served.

After she finished ordering the food and a cold drink for me, she grabbed my hand, stuck it down the front of her blouse, and placed my hand on her chest. I felt a lot of paper, and she said, "Take out whatever you want."

I pulled my hand out, and there I held many one hundred dollar bills. I asked Rebecca where she got them. Doris's voice cut in and said that they went to the bank that day and drew out three thousand dollars from Rebecca's account. I spoke directly to Rebecca and asked her why she drew out so much money. She told me she didn't know why except to say that she felt compelled to do it, and she wanted me to have it. I stated I did not want it and insisted she put the money back in her bra because many of the people in the restaurant were staring at her because she was causing a scene. I asked her who her two friends were, and she said she had just met them and didn't know who they were.

I was very concerned about Rebecca's safety, so I told her I would walk her to her car once we were finished eating. She claimed she didn't remember where her car was, and she had to drive her new friends home. I didn't think that was a very good idea, and I ordered her friends to call a cab. Her friends were not very happy that I came on too strong. They were, after all, strangers to Rebecca and me, and I wasn't sure if they could be trusted. I took Rebecca home and waited until she was safely in the house.

She called me the next day to let me know she got her car and asked if I knew why she had so much money stuffed in her bra. I reiterated what she told me last night. "You said you went to the bank to draw the money out, and you wanted me to have it." She then asked me if I needed it. I emphatically told her that I didn't need it, and I wanted her to put it back in the bank before she lost it.

« *XXIII* »

Doris's Last Day on Earth

Approximately two weeks later, we had our next session. Rebecca came to weight class dressed smartly with new clothes and seemed cordial and friendly to everyone. Expectations were high and everyone was anxious to hear what was going on and couldn't wait to get started. Therefore, it was asked if we could skip the scheduled weight class, but I said no because the first item on the agenda was losing weight and the second item was the study class. We held the weight class, and when it ended, we waited for those who were not staying late to leave the building. The rest were positioning themselves around the so-called hot seat, preparing for what was going to take place. Once everyone settled down, Rebecca sat in the hot seat. She said she was comfortable and ready to participate in tonight's session.

It didn't take long for her to enter into a receptive condition after I spoke the words of my opening incantation. Her body relaxed, she drifted very deep into sleep as if she were dead. Without asking how she felt, Doris's voice cut in immediately and said, "I've been here waiting to talk. This poor excuse of a woman is getting away with murder! Not only did she murder me, but she got off scott free from the hit and run accident where a man was killed. Most of you don't understand; she is a murderer!"

I told Doris that I wasn't interested in anything else about Rebecca. I only wanted to know about the two of them. Doris shot back, "I've told you! She murdered me! How many times must I tell you this? I tried to get my revenge by involving her in another tragedy, but she got off without a trace. Well, she is not going to get away with murdering me!"

"Doris, she will get away with it if you don't tell us in detail what happened."

"What do you want me to do?" inquired Doris.

I instructed Doris, "Think back to the day that you no longer existed in real time. In other words, Doris, think back when you woke up on your last physical day on this earth, namely August 16, 1967."

Doris adjusted the host body in the seat and then began to drift back into time. A few minutes went by and she started to talk. "I get up in the morning and start my day off with a good shower. I can feel it now. It's so warm and refreshing and then I pat myself down with a big fluffy towel. I put on my undergarments and then sit down at my heart-shaped mirror to put on my makeup and a few pieces of jewelry. I decide what I want to wear for the day and I get dressed. Today I have on slacks and a blouse. I don't have anything to eat because I like to wait for the canteen truck at work where I get my coffee and do some socializing. I walked to work today; it seemed to be a good day for that. I met with my co-workers who were also some of my friends just prior to our 7:00 a.m. starting time. I work on an assembly line and get paid for piece work. When the horn blew for our morning coffee break at about 9:30 a.m., we all walked outside in a line to meet the truck."

I interjected a question. "Which coffee company sends the truck to your place?"

Doris said, "He's a young kid named Charlie Manero. Yes! Manero's coffee truck. He has good coffee and sometimes I tease him and tell him that I'd like to dance with him some night at one of the bars." Charlie chuckles and says, "Yea, maybe I'll get lucky, and then he gives me another cup of coffee free of charge."

"We all joke and plan what we will do that evening. A few of the girls asked where I will be going tonight." I responded, "I don't know. Why have you got some place interesting or have you got a hot prospect?"

Just then one of the newer guys said, "I hear that Ma's Place has a new guitar player tonight. Maybe we should go there and listen to him." Doris announced to everyone that it sounded like a good idea.

One of the men hollered, "Hey, Doris, who will you go out with tonight? Jim?"

She shot back, "No, I was with him last night. I don't know who I'll see there tonight; whoever brings me a beer will see me tonight and then maybe the music will keep me there instead of leaving. After a fifteen minute coffee break, we all went back to work. Everybody is chatting about last night's activities and what the prospect of tonight could be.

I never worry because I always have someone to drink with or end the night with lots of lovemaking."

"The day passes on and everyone leaves to go home, and I do the same. I get home, feed the kids, talk with them for a while, then I prepare myself to go out for the evening. Tonight I don't know where I will be or to which bar I will go. I believe it could be Ma's Place. Maybe the new guitarist could be great to listen to."

I added, "How did you get there? Did someone drive you or did you walk?"

Doris responds, "I feel good tonight; I'm a little excited and I don't know why. I think I'll walk to Ma's Place because I like to hear the sound of my heels clicking on the pavement. As I walk, I usually swing my hips and get whistles from young men. This hypes me up because it feels good being a woman. As I approached the bar, I could hear the guitar music and it sounded good to me. I opened the door and went in; the place was packed and the bar was lined up with men. I made my usual walk behind the men sitting at the bar saying hello to some and putting my arms around a few, giving them a kiss on their lips. Half way down the bar, I stared to look way down the end, and it was her; the one who killed me. I got jittery and was bewildered. How could she be there and I'm not dead. I see her clearly. Just then some of the gang insisted that I get on the bar and do a dance for them."

"Before I knew it, I was picked up and put on the bar, and someone removed my shoes and the music was inviting, so I got up and did a shimmy dance up and down the bar. Everyone was whistling and hollering and clapping their hands to the tune of the music. I was enjoying myself dancing as much as they did watching me. I remember doing two dances, and when I was helped down from the bar, I looked down the end and she was not there.

Everybody was also watching the baseball game on television. I had a few beers at the bar and talked with the bartender and some friends."

The guitar music from the other side of the bar sounded good, so I decided to go into the next room. I felt like dancing; the music was very inviting and good for slow, sexy dancing. I grabbed one of the men sitting at the table and asked if he wanted to dance with me. He was a little unstable and so was I. I loved slow dancing because it would put me in a lovable mood. I hung on to my partner and enjoyed the dance. The music ended for a break, and I went back to the bar to catch the baseball score and have another beer. About twenty minutes later, the music continued, and I went back into the dining area and saw a good friend of mine sitting alone. I went over and coaxed him to dance. He was a beautiful dancer – real slow and sexy. I danced two dances with him. On one of the dances, he dipped my body swaying with the music and, of all people, I almost fell into the arms of her – the one who killed me. After the dance he wanted to sit down for a drink, but I had other ideas. I wanted to go parking. I felt sexy and in the mood to make love. I had to practically pull him out of his chair, and we walked out going past Rebecca who was sitting by the door and staring at me.

We got into his car and headed down Main Street to South Street to the parking area at the Duck Pond. We sat there hugging, petting, talking, and drinking a beer. I was in the mood for romance, and he wanted wild lusty sex. We argued, and he started the car and told me he was upset that I let him drive all the way out here, and we didn't have sex. I told him that's no so; I just wanted to talk a while. I didn't stop him from petting me. I was just not hot enough and ready to participate the way he wanted to – like an animal. He sped up the road with the wheels screeching on the hot top. The window was open, and I took off my shoes and threw them out of the window. I enjoyed the cool breeze and felt like I wanted to sleep for a while.

My friend asked me where my shoes were. I admitted that I threw them out the window. He wanted to know why. I explained that I just felt like it; I wanted to be bare foot. He got upset with me and warned he would stop the car and throw me out. Not taking him seriously, I told him to do it because I wanted to get out. He stopped the car and reached over me to open the door and yelled at me to get out, as he pushed me out. I fell to the ground on my knees, as he drove away and the door slammed shut. I got up and brushed my dress off and cursed him.

Here I was, under the weather, walking wobbly and staggering in the middle of the night. It's pitch black, and I heard a car coming up from behind. As the car slowly approached me, the passenger side window came down.

There she was! Rebecca was driving the car and asked me if I was all right. I told her I was okay, and my friend was a jerk throwing me out of the car. Rebecca offered me a ride back to the bar, but I told her I would rather be taken home. Rebecca ordered me to get in the car, and I did. I was tired and unsteady, and Rebecca drove on, and, before I knew it, I was sound asleep. When I woke up, it felt like hours had gone by, and I asked Rebecca why she stopped the car. We were not at my house but had stopped in a field near a body of water.

Rebecca reached over and put her hand on my right breast and attempted to pull me close to her. I urged her to stop and take me home. She argued with me and warned me to stay still; she wanted to hug me and kiss me. I hollered, NO! Stop it, I want to go home! She shook my body and again insisted that I stay still so she could kiss me. We struggled and she gave me a left hook to my jaw, and I was stunned. I could still hear her words, "I only wanted to hug and kiss you; this didn't have to happen." Angrily, she got out of the car and slammed the door. She proceeded around the front of the car and opened the door on my side. She grabbed my arms and threw my body back on the car seat and pulled my dress up. She pulled my silk stocking off my leg and dragged me out of the car down on the ground. She straddled her body over me and wrapped the stocking around my throat. We struggled and fought, and then my body went limp. The last thing I remembered was when she grabbed my sterling necklace and I heard her say, "You won't need this anymore," and she pulled it from my neck. I felt like I was floating and saw her drive away.

Doris became restless in Rebecca's body and she said, "I want to leave; I'm confused."

Rebecca woke up from the trance and said that this was the first time she felt uncomfortable and wanted to go home. She got up and excused herself and supposedly went home.

The group had all kinds of questions, and a discussion continued for a few hours. The big question was whether it really happened the way Doris told the story. She didn't reveal the name of who she left the café with and, even when she was thrown out of the car, we thought she would have been mad enough to call his name, yet, she did say she was under the influence of alcohol. I told everyone not to try to solve the mystery, but to go home and sleep on it, and when we meet next time, we could attempt to put an answer together. Do we have a frantic woman in Rebecca who believes a spirit named Doris is attempting to destroy her, or is the spirit of Doris really present and tormenting Rebecca to a point of destroying herself? Rebecca believes Doris is haunting her, and she can't do anything without being affected by her spirit. Rebecca claims Doris's spirit is getting stronger and is commanding her to do things in the physical plane, such as drinking, buying smaller clothes, driving recklessly, and spending money by forcing her to use her credit cards. Doris claims she will get revenge on Rebecca for strangling her to death.

«*XXIV*»

A Dying Woman's Confession

About two weeks passed, and I was working in my office late one night when I heard loud footsteps on my front stairs. I turned to look at the clock on the wall and saw that it was 2:10 a.m. At that moment, this person began knocking frantically. I got up and opened the door and there was Rebecca standing there looking tattered and disheveled. I opened the conversation. "Hi, Rebecca; how come you're out so late?"

Rebecca replied, "I couldn't sleep, so I decided to ride around a bit before deciding to stop by and see you."

I asked, "Are you okay? You look a little pale."

"Can I come in or do I have to stand out here all night? Are you afraid of me?" Rebecca sarcastically asked.

Calmly I said, "No, I'm not afraid of you. By all means, come in. Go right to the rear office or just sit out here in the front room."

Rebecca sat down in the chair in the front room, and she let out a big sigh.

I continued, "Okay, Rebecca, what is on your mind? Why did you want to talk to me?"

"I don't know what's happening to me," said Rebecca. "I feel a little mixed up and confused. I keep hearing things and doing things that don't make sense."

I asked, "Like what Rebecca? Give me an example."

Trying to understand as well, Rebecca said, "It's hard to explain. I feel a little confused; let me think."

"Take your time," I responded. "Just relax and let the words flow out. Just try."

Still confused, Rebecca continued, "I'll try (she coughs). I find myself buying size 5 dresses, and I know I wear a size

10-12. I then have to go back and return them. It makes me feel stupid and ridiculous."

"That's kind of odd. Do you have any family members or friends who wear a size 5? Maybe you were thinking of them and possibly went ahead and bought these clothes as gifts for them?"

Rebecca answered, "No, that's not it. I feel kind of spooky about it. I have a strong feeling that the dress belongs to someone I know, but I can't recall the name."

"How often does that happen?"

Rebecca replied, "Too many times; it's uncontrollable. It's the same when I order a drink. I always order vodka or gin mixed, but I find myself ordering beer and drinking it. I don't like beer. It's as if someone spoke to me in my head and made me order the beer. It's crazy!"

"Who do you think is telling you to do this?"

"I wish I knew," shouted Rebecca. "It's like someone is haunting me. I can't sleep nights. I feel someone is inside me making me do these things that I don't want to do and I never did before. I feel I've lost control of myself, and it's getting stronger every day that goes by. I need some help, and I don't know where to turn."

"Rebecca," I then asked, "Have you consulted with a medical doctor or a psychiatrist about this?"

Excited, Rebecca yelled, "I'm not nuts, and what the **hell** do doctors know about being haunted, or know about spirits and ghosts?"

Raffaele continued, "Why do you believe that you're being haunted by a spirit?"

Rebecca revealed, "I believe I did something very bad a long time ago. I think I hurt someone. I can still feel my hands around someone's neck, and I'm squeezing harder and harder. I can't stop."

Trying to calm Rebecca, I held her hands and said, "Rebecca, relax; take it easy, breathe deeply, talk slowly, and don't tighten your hands, relax."

Listening to my words, Rebecca replied, "Okay (she sighed and breathed slowly). Sometimes it feels like we are two people in one body. She influences me to use my credit cards, and we go buy a lot of things that I can't use or don't want."

Curious, I asked, "You mention that she influences you. Are the feelings that of a woman inside of you?"

Rebecca affirmed, "Yes, the image and impressions feel very much like a small woman."

"That could very well account for your buying smaller dress sizes – a size 5."

"I can hear her telling me that she is going to haunt me until the truth comes out, and then she will have her revenge and get even with me for what I did to her," continued Rebecca.

Frustrated, I asked, "Just what the hell is the truth, Rebecca?"

She sadly told me, "The truth, Raffaele, is that I am dying. I have terminal cancer, and I was told I only have five years to live. That is what I get from my doctors; that's all they know. There is nothing they can do for me."

Surprised, I said, "I'm sorry to hear that news Rebecca. Are you sure? Did you get a second opinion?"

Rebecca replied, "I'm sure the doctors are right when it comes to illness like this, but enough of me and my cancer. I must confide in you because I feel I can trust you."

"What is it? What is so important that you must tell me now?"

Rebecca demanded, "First, you must promise me that you won't tell anyone, including the authorities, until I'm dead and buried in the ground for at least <u>five</u> years."

Surprised by her request, I refuted, "You're talking through your head, Rebecca. You're not going to die. Many people have overcome cancer and so will you....if you're determined and strong willed."

Almost pleading, Rebecca cried, "I certainly will die within the next five years, and then you must wait another five years before you reveal what I am about to tell you. It could be devastating to some."

"I don't know if I can promise you that I will wait that long."

Rebecca snapped, "Then I won't tell you what I believe I did. It will be the story of your life. It will be the truth and nobody else will have it except you and your associate."

I agreed, "Okay Rebecca. I'll make you that promise. I will not reveal anything that you tell me tonight for at least <u>five</u> years after you have died and have been buried. Is that what you want from me?"

Relieved, Rebecca sighed, "Yes, that's what I want. Now let me tell you this. I believe the spirit of a girl that **I killed** many years ago is haunting me. Her spirit seems to have the ability to become one with me when she enters my body. It's like two people in one body. No matter what I do. I can't get rid of her. It's driving me insane."

I'm stunned. "Wow, that is wild! Who did you kill?"

"I'm not sure," Rebecca replied. "I believe her name was Doris."

"How can you prove that you did this?"

Rebecca answered, "I have many flashbacks of the incident over and over; it won't stop. I can't stand it any longer."

Questioning the validity of Rebecca's confession, I asked her, "You're not making this up, are you, Rebecca?"

"Why would I lie about something as serious as this?" she protested. Rebecca went on to explain, "I remember hitting her then dragging her to the edge of the car seat. I lifted her dress up so I could pull her silk stocking off and then I wrapped it around her pretty neck. I then choked her, strangled her and dragged her body to the river's edge. Oh yes! I also remember pulling some jewelry off her neck. I can still see her bruised face and her half naked body lying in the water. Although I knew she couldn't hear me, I told her she wouldn't have any use for the necklace anymore. I blamed her for what had happened. If she only cooperated and let me kiss her. I then went blank and forgot everything until I got involved with you."

"Why are you telling me all of this?"

Sincerely, Rebecca answered, "I trust you. You've always been honest with me."

"How do you know I won't go to the police?" I emphasized.

Rebecca insisted, "You won't go to the authorities because you promised me you would not tell anyone about this for five years. I will show you something that will convince you that I was <u>the killer</u>."

Still curious, I asked, "What could you show me to convince me that you strangled her?"

Rebecca opened her handbag and reached in and slowly pulled out a necklace of some sort. She held it in her hand and said, "You see this Raffaele? I pulled it off her neck. She didn't need it anymore." Rebecca dangled the necklace over the palm of my hand, and she let it fall. The necklace was now in my possession.

"How do I know this is Doris's and not a trinket from the Five and Dime Store and you're not making this up?" I questioned.

Excited, Rebecca screamed, "It's the truth! Just like I will be dead and buried within five years."

Tired and exhausted, I suggested to Rebecca, "I think you should go home and get a good night's sleep, and let me think about what you just told me."

Again Rebecca warned, "Do not forget I got your promise – nothing to be revealed until I'm dead and buried for at least five years after my death. I'm going to hold you to your trust and word. Don't let me reach you from the great beyond like I've been haunted by Doris."

Rebecca left that night and never came back to any of the classes. As time went by, I heard from Rebecca about twice a month. She would call me to let me know how she was holding up. After that last meeting, she never discussed

Doris with me again. It was as if the case was closed and Doris never existed. Rebecca got involved helping the less fortunate. She helped at the soup kitchens, and saw to it that the people who couldn't get out had food delivered to them. It was as if her whole life had changed for the better. She had been a frequent cancer patient of the local hospital, and you could see that as time went by she was failing.

I received a few calls from her while she was hospitalized. I even went to visit her towards the end of her illness, and it was difficult seeing her wane away. We never mentioned Doris's name. Then one night I got a call from her while she was still in the hospital, and she sounded weak and frail.

That was the last time she said to me, "Remember your promise to me, Raffaele...at least five years. I may not be talking to you anymore. Please remember me. I really wasn't such a bad person."

I heard a click on the other end, and that was the last time I heard from her. The last time I saw Rebecca, she was lying in a coffin.

About the Authors

Raffaele J. Bibbo is a civil engineer and registered land surveyor. He has studied the spiritual world for most of his life and has experienced many contacts with spirits. He has also lectured and demonstrated on the subject and has appeared on numerous television programs as well as radio. Raffaele has also produced and directed several short programs for the local cable network. *Spirits Surround Us* was his first publication.

Diane M. Marobella has been studying, researching, and investigating the spiritual phenomena for the last fifteen years. As an administrative assistant in her professional life, she has also assisted in recording and maintaining data for the many cases in which she has been involved. As co-author of *Haunted by the Spirit*, this is her first endeavor in the field of writing.

Printed in the United States
1006800002B

9 781403 396815